EVELINE SCOTT

Bedtime Stories For Kids

Your Magical Manual To Help Your Kid's Imagination... Evening After Evening!

Table of Contents

Dina and the Dinos

Every night it was Dina's job to take out the garbage after dinner. Her brother and sister would help clear the table and wash the dishes. One evening, Dina heard what sounded like meowing from behind the garbage cans. She saw a hungry Mommy cat and two kittens.

Feeling bad for the kitties, Dina decided to feed them leftovers from dinner. And for the next few nights, the family of cats would wait for her to bring them something to eat. Eventually, the cats got scared away by a group of hungry raccoons. They left an awful mess as they ripped open the garbage bags looking for some sweet treats. The following night Dina noticed that there were no animals outside at all. "How strange," she thought as she headed back inside the house. Other than a few crickets chirping, the night was still and quiet. A few hours later, while Dina was fast asleep, she heard many loud banging noises outside. Did the animals she used to feed come back for more? She knew she should've stayed inside, but she was curious to see who or what was making all that racket.

Dina was not prepared for what she was about to see. Waiting for her outside was a dinosaur, a baby dinosaur! It had to be a dream.

"I just need to close my eyes and go back to sleep," she told herself. That was until the dinosaur gave her a big sloppy kiss. Yep, this was happening. The baby dinosaur began to whimper like a puppy. He wanted Dina to follow him. "I can't go with you, boy. I have to go back to bed." He looked at her with his big sweet eyes, and she couldn't refuse. "Ok. Maybe just a few minutes. But then I have to go back inside." Dina continued to follow the baby dinosaur that she named "Dino." "Where are you taking me?" she wondered. "That's far enough. I have to get back now." Unfortunately, she was now lost.

How long had she been walking? Everything looked different around her. Where was she? It was so humid. It felt like they were in a jungle. Maybe that was because they were in a wilderness! Dina felt a little afraid but couldn't help to admire how beautiful the scenery was. The quiet was soon disturbed by some big thumping noises. The baby dinosaur ran off towards the noise. "Hey? Where are you going? There were giant dinosaurs everywhere. The baby dinosaur ran over to what must've been his Mommy and Daddy. He seemed very happy to be with them as they nuzzled against him. It was kind of cute to watch them together. The Mommy dinosaur walked over to Dina, which scared her at first. But then she saw how gentle the dinosaur was.

She wanted to feed Dina some grass. "No thanks. I already had dinner," she told the dinosaur. These dinosaurs were called Brontosauruses. From what she remembered in school, they only ate plants, which came as a relief. It was good to know that she wasn't going to be on the menu that day. They treated her like I was one of their own. "Oh, hi there, little guy. I know you. You're a Raptor. Well, aren't you cutest little thing." He growled at her, but he was still just a baby, so it was more of a grumble. As Dina continued to talk to him, she could feel a group of eyes looking at her. She started to feel very uncomfortable. Before she knew it, Dina was surrounded by hungry Raptors. They were mean and vicious. Things didn't look suitable for Dina when an older man dressed in rags came to her rescue. He was pudgy and had a big bushy grey beard. Not precisely a dashing hero.

He was able to fend off the Raptors with a stick. "Who are you?" Dina asked. "I'll tell you later. Here's the plan... run as fast as you can!" "That's your plan?" "Uh, yeah," the old man said as the two began to run through the jungle. "We just need to make it to the waterfall," the old man shouted. "Waterfall?" The pair were somehow able to elude the Raptors and made it to the waterfall. "Can you swim?" asked the old man. "Yeah, why...oh no!" "I have a raft waiting for us at the bottom of this cliff." "No way!" Dina emphatically said. Then she saw the angry eyes and sharp teeth of the Raptors getting closer. She jumped.

Miraculously the pair survived their big plunge into the river. Unfortunately, the older man got his legs trapped in some seaweed at the bottom. Dina didn't notice that he was trapped, and neither one of them noticed that they weren't alone. A giant dinosaur from the deep was heading their way. Things did not look suitable for the duo. Then, from out of nowhere, some fish swam by, distracting the sea monster. The older man could get his legs free, and the two swam as fast as they could towards the surface.

Soaked, exhausted, and still shook up by almost being eaten by dinosaurs, the pair finally made it to shore. "We'll be safe in my cave. I have food and fire, so we'll be fine until morning," the old man told Dina. She wasn't listening. She was scared, tired, and she just wanted to go home. She still had no idea how she ended up here or who this older man was. "I know you want to go home, kid, as do I. My name is Dr. Darwin Slate.

I'm a scientist. I've always been fascinated with time travel. One day I discovered a time portal. I walked inside of it, and I've been stuck here ever since. How'd you end up here?" "I followed a baby dinosaur into the woods," Dina replied.

"What??????" "I have been looking for that portal for weeks, months, maybe even longer. I don't know how long I've been here. Do you remember where it was?" "I think so. It was in the area where you saved me from those Raptors." "Fantastic! Get some sleep, for tomorrow will be a long day. Hopefully, one where we will both find our way home." "Our 'taxis' have arrived. Hold on tight and enjoy the scenery."

Waiting for us with a group of brontosauruses, including one special little one. "Dino!" Dina yelled as she saw her little dinosaur friend. "Things could get dangerous, so be brave, and we'll find that portal and be very soon," Dr. Slate tried to reassure Dina and himself. "Don't worry about the Pterodactyls overhead. They're too high up, and they don't see us. Hey, did you know that the "P" is silent? Isn't that p-funny?" Silence. Dina didn't react. "Guess it's too early for dinosaur jokes this morning." "They look so familiar," Dina said as she looked at a group of dinosaurs chewing on some plants and vegetables.

"They're called Stegosauruses. They aren't dangerous but let's not get too close. I wouldn't want to feel those sharp spikes on their back," Dr. Slate commented. A loud rumbling noise is starting to get closer and closer. It was a group of Triceratops. "Keep still. They won't eat us, but you don't want to get poked by those sharp horns," Dr. Slate whispered. "We're almost there. I recognize this area," Dina told the doctor.

"Looks like our old friends, the Raptors, are waiting for us," Dr. Slate said. "What are we going to do?" Dina wondered. "I brought some food. Hopefully, it will distract them. Uh oh! Did you feel that?" "Feel what?" Dina replied. "We're in trouble now. Huge trouble!" "Tyrannosaurus Rex! The most feared dinosaur of them all!" Dr. Slate started to panic. "This is one dinosaur that does want to eat us." Frozen with fear, neither the doctor nor Dina could move a muscle. But an unlikely hero would emerge.

"Dino! No!" Dina shouted as the little dinosaur went to protect his friends. He was too small and ended up being hurt by the T-Rex. "Let me try something," Doctor Slate said as he tossed some meat in the T-Rex's direction. The group of Raptors swarmed the T-Rex looking for more to eat. They buzzed around the T-Rex, who just swatted them like mosquitoes. It gave Dr. Slate and Dina a chance to escape. "I want to see if he's ok!" Dina screamed.

"We have to go now! The time warp could close at any moment!" Slate shouted, taking her by the hand. She looked back one last time to see Dino's mom looking over her injured baby. "Earth to Dina! Hello!" "Sorry, Lola, I must've dozed off during the tour of The Museum of Science." "Well, I hope my tour hasn't been that boring," a familiar voice said. "Dr. Slate?" "Have we met before?" he replied. "I guess you just look like someone I know," Dina said, a little disappointed. "Oh, by the way, the baby dinosaur is going to be just fine," Dr. Slate said with a wink and a smile before walking away. A smile started to form on Dina's lips. Whether or not any of this happened, it was one heck of a ride.

The Magic Gold Button

Once there was a kid named Philip. He was a brilliant and naughty kid. He loves adventure. He has a hobby that he used to go in the woods ordinarily without fail. He was curious about witches and magic. He always wonders if these things were real or not.

Philip was five years old when he used to have faith in powerful things, for example, witches. But what to do, his companions never trusted in what he said. They all felt that he was becoming frantic as he was developing older. But Philip used to disregard them and accepted that one day he would demonstrate that there are things, for example, witches.

One day as he was strolling in the woodlands. Philip shockingly found a magic button. He was at a distance from the button when he saw the button was moving. At first, he got scared, but then he became curious and started moving towards the button. When he reached near the button, it jumps into his hand. It was a shiny gold button. He first thinks to drop the button and return home, but then something weird happened. The button gets a bit shinier, and within no time, the forest was changed into a city.

Without a moment's delay, he got the contemplations that this was the place of a witch, which later ended up being right. There was a house in front of him, which neither disappeared in the forest and even it was at its place in the city as well.

When he glanced through the window, he saw an older woman making something in a significant dark pot. She was adding some frightful fixings like the tongue of a toad, the eye of a newt, and a hand of a dead cat. He shrugged at this sight. However, Philip chose to stay. At that point, she called her giant dark feline and requested that it bring the powder called "invisibility powder." But as the cat was not smart like a human, it got an appeal called "dwarf charm." The lady, not seeing the name, poured the entire of it into the pot.

She requested that the spoon mix, and it began mixing it. The coin once again starts getting shinny. There were some blasts, fireworks and Philip twisted down to save himself. When it was all over, he raised his heads and saw something which was amazingly astounding.

By now, you probably thought about the thing I am talking about. The witch had changed into a mouse. At first, Philip didn't understand what happened. Still, when he understood it, it made him giggle as quite a while past individuals chuckled at the motion pictures of Charlie Chaplin. There was a black cat in the house, and it might be the witch's pet. The cat was seemed hungry for days; when he saw the mouse, his mouth watered, and he ate the mouse (the witch).

Then the cat sleeps in his bed. Philip looks at the coin, but it has vanished. He tries to find it but couldn't. Then he steps outside the house, and everything was back to normal. He heads toward his home and never forgets the whole scene. He tries to tell others about the incident, but they think he might be lying, so he stops telling others about it.

Magic Land

For centuries, a small village made up of elves, fairies, and a kindly old gnome has secretly existed without anyone knowing. It is a beautiful place where everyone feels like one big family. Magic Land is filled with happiness, charity, and love. Everyone in Magic Land loves and respects nature. They share all of the food and resources with each other and the animals who call the forest home. It seemed as though life couldn't get any better for the friendly citizens of Magic Land.

Unfortunately, that was all about to change. Thurston Prescott was a wealthy businessman. Today he took his son Edward or Ed, as he preferred, to the park by the forest. Thurston spent most of the time on his phone while Ed kicked a ball around. Ed kicked the ball so hard that it disappeared into a group of trees. Ed found his ball but decided to keep walking more in-depth into the forest. As he turned to walk back to the car, he saw what looked to be an elf picking berries. "Hello?" Frightened, the elf didn't know what to say. "What's your name? I'm Ed" "Oh no!" the elf thought, "It's a human!"

Soon the elf was joined by his fellow villagers. "Hi everyone! My name is Ed. You sure have a beautiful little town here." "What do we do now?" asked one of the fairies. "Let's bring him to the Gnome," suggested the elf. The Gnome always knows what to do."

16

And so, Ed followed his mini-escorts into the woods. Ed was greeted by the rest of the elves and fairies before the Gnome arrived. "Hello Ed, and welcome to Magic Land. You are more than welcome to join us for lunch. All we ask is that you respect everyone and everything you see around you." Then they all feasted on every type of berry you can imagine. "Ed! Ed!" came a voice from behind the trees.

"Uh oh! It's my Dad." "Quick everybody, hide!" whispered the Gnome. Ed's Dad arrived and was amazed by what he saw. "Look at this place. Just imagine what I could do with all this land." He then picked up his phone and started to dial. Ed was unfortunate during the car ride home as he worried about his tiny new pals and what would happen to their village. "So, tomorrow morning, I want to tear down the forest and start building right away. We're going to make a fortune!" Ed felt so helpless as he listened to his Dad planning to destroy the forest and Magic Land.

"Friends, I have just heard some terrible news," began the Gnome. "Humans are planning to get rid of our happy little village. There will be big trucks here. We are peaceful and don't like to fight. When the time comes, we will be left with no choice but to release the bees". "Let me know when you're ready to go, Mr. Prescott." "Will do. Isn't this exciting, Ed? It is going to make me lots and lots of money!" his Dad boasted. Ed just stood and tried not to cry.

He had to stop this from happening, but he didn't know-how. But he couldn't just stand by and do nothing. The swarm of bees and elves were no match for the mighty machines. It looked as though it would take a miracle to save Magic Land from the bulldozers. Without warning, Ed ran out in front of the devices before they reached the trees.

Whether Mr. Prescott was moved by his Ed's bravery (or maybe the fairy dust was doing the trick), he ordered the bulldozers to stop. "I'm so sorry, Ed. I have been so selfish. I put money ahead of my son. I'm going to make sure that this forest is protected forever." Ed was a hero! He had saved Magic Land! And if that wasn't enough, Mr. Prescott kept his promise to Ed There would be no hotels, casinos, or any concrete poured in Magic Land. The only ones allowed to enjoy this fantastic little place were a group of elves, fairies, and a wise old gnome. And, of course, a brave young man who was welcome anytime.

It is Ivy Cottage

And this is Freddie and Jimmy. Early on a winter morning, Freddie and Jimmy woke up with a yawn. Jimmy opened one eye, then the other, and Freddie stretched. Their owners were nowhere to be seen. But Jimmy had noticed that something was wrong. "Freddie, Freddie," he cried, "The world has disappeared." Freddie just laughed. "You silly kitten," he said, "the world has not disappeared. It is just covered with snow."

In an instant, Freddie hatched a plan. A fascinating plan. A program like no other plan he had ever hatched before. "I am not sure I like the sound of this," mumbled Jimmy as he followed Freddie out of the cat flap. At first, Jimmy did not like the cold feeling on his paws or the icy surface on his whiskers.

"I want to go home and curl up by the fire." he mewed.

But Freddie was already over by the pond calling Jimmy to come and have a look. So, Jimmy walked carefully across the crunchy snow, around the rockery, down where the path usually was, over the herb garden, and towards the pond.

When he got there, he found something strange. Something extraordinary. Something extraordinary indeed. Freddie was sta nding on the pond. Not in it. On it! Freddie was sliding around on the ice where the pond had frozen. "Weeeeeeeeeeee!" he cried as he spun around. "Are you sure that is a good idea?" Jimmy asked. Suddenly there was a loud crack as the ice broke! Freddie scrambled to the side of the pond, slipping and sliding towards Jimmy. Luckily, he escaped just as the ice sunk to the bottom of the pond.

"I told you that was a bad idea," said Jimmy, but Freddie was already off on another adventure. "Come on," he yelled excitedly. "I am not sure about this," repeated Jimmy.

By the time Jimmy caught up with Freddie, he had already made a big ball of snow. "Watch this!" Freddie cried and sent the ball rolling and tumbling down the hill. When the snowball thudded into the fence at the bottom of the mountain, it was massive. "Again, again!" yelled Freddie as he sent down another ball of crisp, white snow.

Freddie and Jimmy chased the snowballs down to where they had crashed into the fence. The second one was not as big as the first, and it gave Freddie an idea... "Let's make a snowcat!" Together they heaved the smaller snowball onto the bigger one. They then made some ears, legs, and long tails and found some sticks that looked just like whiskers. Soon they had made a handsome snow-cat.

As they finished the snowcat, Jimmy noticed it was getting dark. Heavy flakes of snow were falling from the sky. Jimmy's paws were cold, his tail was wet, and icicles were starting to hang from his whiskers. "I want to go home," he cried. So, they set off for home. They went past the frozen pond, over the herb garden, down where the path usually was, around the rockery until they were safely back home. "I am worn out." yawned Jimmy as they climbed through the cat flap at Ivy Cottage. "So am I.," said Freddie. So, they curled up in their favorite place by the fire and drifted off to sleep just as their owners came home. "Oh, what a lazy pair," they said. "I bet you've done nothing all day."

Drago

Drago Makes a Friend

Drago lived in a big, dark, gloomy cave on the darker, more tragic Dark Mountainside. Drago was a dragon. The scaly lizard was giant than a barn.

Drago did not have many friends. Most people never walked on the darker side of Dark Mountain. When Drago did see people, they usually screamed and ran away.

At first, Drago had tried to be nice, "Hi, I am Drago." The dragon would put on his best smile. "It doesn't matter what you do," Drago's brother Steven would say, "People don't like dragons, and dragons don't like people." Drago did not want to believe Steven. There must be some people who would talk to dragons. But after years of trying, Drago stopped striving to be excellent. "If they don't like me, then I won't like them!" Drago said after scaring off some hikers. He had given the hikers his best angry-faced screech. He was sulking as he looked through the picnic basket that the hikers had left behind.

"Well, that isn't an excellent attitude," said a little voice that Drago could not see. The dragon looked all around, but he could not know the maker of that sound. "I am down here!" She said, patting the dragon on the leg. Drago jumped back when he felt the little hand touch his leg. "My name is Emily, and I don't think what you did is nice." Drago did not know what to say. He had waited his whole life to talk to a human. "Well, people always just scream," Drago started. "Even if I smile and say hi, they shriek and run away." Continued a worked-up dragon.

He wanted Emily to understand that he was not mean. Drago could tell that Emily was not convinced. The little girl did not believe that there was a good reason to be mean to people. "How will you make friends if you are mean to everyone?" asked the little girl. "I do not have any friends," Drago confessed. He hung his head in shame. "Well, you do now." Emily said, "Here is a friendship bracelet." The young girl put the bracelet on the dragon. The bracelet would only fit on Drago's pinky finger. "Thank you," Drago was amazed; he had never gotten a gift before. "And I will show you how to make more friends." Emily grabbed the dragon by the hand and led him down the mountain. Emily took the dragon down into the valley of Nod.

The two new friends spent the day meeting new people. Some of the people ran away. Many of the people were happy to meet such a friendly dragon. "You see," Emily would say, "You don't have to be mean." Emily walked Drago back to his cave. The friends were excited about the fantastic day they had had. Emily promised Drago that she would be back the next day. Drago went right to bed. He wanted to get a good night's sleep to be ready to play with his friend in the morning. The moral of the story Just be yourself, don't try to be the person you think people want you to be.

Drago Has a Dream

"It must be amazing to be a dragon," Emily would always say. Drago's best friend thought it would be cool to fly around all day. She did not understand the problems that dragons have. Emily believes that being big is easy. "Nobody can boss you around," she would say. Drago did not like being big. "When you are big, people are afraid of you," he explained to Emily. Drago always had to be careful when he walked. His big feet often broke wagons and walls. Drago worried that he was going to hurt someone. "But you can fly!" Emily would say. "That must be so much fun." Drago did like to fly. Sometimes when he passed, he could see for miles. The beautiful ground below was a fantastic sight.

"But when I fly, people scream," Drago told Emily. The villagers did not like to see something as big as Drago flying through the sky. "I do not like being a dragon." Emily could see that her big dragon friend was upset. It was getting late, and Emily had to go home. So, the young girl told the dragon that she would come back and visit tomorrow. Drago laid down in his pile of straw. He closed his eyes. "I don't want to be a dragon," he mumbled as he drifted off to sleep. All of a sudden, Drago found himself in the center of town. The buildings looked much more significant than average. The people were also much more extensive than usual. They were all about the same size as Drago. "How do you do?" A young man asked Drago politely. Villagers walked all around Drago.

Nobody seemed upset or terrified by his presence. The dragon decided to take a walk downtown. He talked to a few people about the weather.

Drago enjoyed being normal. The dragon saw Emily walking through the market, and he went to say hi. "Who are you?" Emily said to Drago. Emily walked away from the normal-sized Drago. The dragon walked a little further, and his feet started to get tired. He tried to jump up and fly. Drago was ready to rise in the air.

Instead, he landed with a thud on the ground. Drago became very hungry. He decided to find some food.

There was a hot- dog cart just down the road. The owner told Drago that he had no hotdogs to sell because his grill was not working. Drago told the man that he could cook the hotdogs. The man put three hotdogs on the grill.

Drago took a deep breath before attempting to breathe fire. No fire came out.

Drago walked back to his cave hungry, tired, and lonely. That is when Drago awoke from his nap. He looked at himself. He stared around the room. "Phew!" The dragon exclaimed, "I am still a dragon."

The moral of the story Be yourself. Everyone wants to be someone else from time to time, but you have to work on being the best you can be. Each one of us has our unique talents and abilities.

Dragon-Sized Fire Sneezes

Emily and Drago were walking past a meadow that was filled with beautiful orange flowers. Emily picked one flower to put in her hair. Drago told Emily that it looked very nice. As they continued to walk, Drago paused. His face started to twitch. Drago could feel a tickly kind of pressure in his head as he let out a gigantic, "AHHH-CHEEEW!" The sneeze was so loud that Emily dropped to the ground. When she looked up, the meadow was completely burned up. "Drago, are you ok?" Emily asked.

There was no answer. She looked around the meadow and saw Drago in a tree a mile down the road. Drago tried to get out, but he was stuck. Emily ran over to help her friend. When Emily got to the tree, Drago started to make a funny noise. "Aaa-ggg," he said. "Aaa-ggg, Aaaa-aaachewww!" Emily was sent flying backward.

Hen, she got back to her feet, a black spot on the ground where the tree had been. The dragon was nowhere in sight.

Emily looked down the road. She spotted Drago.

He was stuck halfway through a barn roof. Emily ran down the road to see her friend. When Emily got there, many farmers were standing around debating how to get the dragon out of their barn. "I am stuck," Drago said as Emily got closer. "What did you say?" Emily asked as she reached the barn.

"Aaa-ggg, Aaaaaa-aaachewww!" The dragon sneezed so loud all of the farmers were sent flying into the pasture. Emily was blown into a pile of hay. Her hat fell into a puddle; she stood herself up and dusted herself off. Emily began to look around for her friend Drago. The whole roof of the barn had been burned away. The little girl saw Drago lying flat on his back in a field. Emily ran to see if her friend was ok. "Don't come near me," the dragon said as Emily got closer. "I am too dangerous." Drago just laid flat on his back. He did not want to risk any more fiery sneezes.

Emily walked over to the dragon anyway. She held her friend's hand to comfort him. "I am going to have to leave forever." Drago complained, "Nobody can be around a dragon that cannot control his sneezes." After a little while, Emily said, "Well, you aren't sneezing now." The dragon realized that he had stopped sneezing. He did not even feel a sneezy tickle. Then one of the farmers walked over with Emily's hat. Emily took the cap and put it on her head.

"Aaa-aaa," Drago started. Emily threw the hat as far away as she could. Drago's sneeze stopped. "I cannot stay. It is too dangerous for you if I do." Drago said as he stretched out his wings. "But it stopped," Emily said to her friend. "It was the flower on my hat that made you sneeze," Emily explained. "You are allergic." Drago was relieved to find out that he could control his horrible sneezes. The dragon was also happy that he did not have to leave. The two friends continued on their walk without any more sneezes.

Moral of the story

Never give up on true friendship. Help others when they need it the most!

Drago and the Present

Drago was excited today. His best friend Emily was coming over to play at three o'clock. Drago was excited to see Emily. When they last talked, Emily, told Drago that she had a present for him. Drago loved presents.

"Emily is so very thoughtful," the large dragon thought to himself. He looked at the clock on his wall. It read noon.

Drago knew he had a long time before Emily got there. He decided to clean his room. After he finished cleaning his room, Drago checked the clock for a second time.

The clock still said noon. The dragon decided that he would clean his whole cave. "That will take a long time," Drago said as he tried to get himself motivated. The dragon got started by picking up all of his stinky socks from the living room floor after picking up the smelly socks, washing the dishes, and sweeping every bed in the entire cave. Drago went back to his clock to check the time. Once again, the clock had not moved. Drago was getting very upset. "Why will you not move!?" The angry dragon yelled at

31

the clock. Emily was never going to get there if the clock would not help. "You have to say three o'clock before Emily can come and play with me."

The dragon was very concerned. Drago needed to come up with an extended plan. He needed to find a job that would take long enough for his clock to turn to three o'clock. Drago decided that he would take everything out of his cave. Then once everything was out, he would put it all back in again. Drago knew this would take him a long time and so he started by carrying out the couch. Drago does not have a traditional sofa.

His couch is made for dragons. It weighs 9,000 pounds.

Drago lifted one end as he started to drag the couch out of his cave. The heavy piece of furniture dragged along the ground. As soon as he had it outside, he continued to remove more and more furniture out of the cave. Drago set down the coffee table, and he was about to go and get more when he heard. "What is going on here?" Drago turned around to see Emily standing right behind him. "I was just trying to do some cleaning and pass the time until you got here."

The dragon told his friend. Emily had the gift in her hand, and Drago got so excited he sat down on his outdoor couch to open it. "A clock?" The dragon said as he pulled it out of the gift bag. "Well, I knew that your clock was broken," Emily said as Drago's mouth hit the floor. His clock was broken. All of a sudden, Drago realized that he had been cleaning all day. He looked at all of his furniture spread out in front of his cave. The giant, the silly dragon, was very tired. He stretched out on his couch to take a nap.

Moral of the story

Stop to think. Ask questions if something seems strange. There is nothing wrong with asking questions!

The Great Dragon Race

Drago was nervous when he woke up. Today was the day of the Great Dragon Race. Dragons and humans from all over the country would be coming to see two dragons' races. Drago was racing his big brother Steven. The winner would get to stay at his home, and the loser would have to leave to find a new home. The area was big enough for both dragons. They had lived there together for years. Now that they were older, the territory was getting too crowded.

Drago was worried that he would have to find a new place to live. He liked living on Dark Mountain and flying through the Valley of Nod. It had been his only home. Emily was another problem. What if Drago never saw her again? Drago had never had a friend like Emily. She was the first person to see him and not immediately run away. The dragon master, Zigoto, had come from Dragon Mountain to judge the race. Zigoto was the wisest of all the dragons.

He ordered the referees to blast the ram's horn. Drago and Steven knew that it was time to get to the starting line. "It will be ok," said Emily as she came walking up the mountain. Drago ran over to see his friend. "You can't be here," he said to the little girl. "This is only for dragons." But Drago could tell that Emily was not going anywhere. "I am here to cheer you on," Emily said as she hugged her dragon friend. Drago found Emily a place to watch the race out of sight.

Drago went to the starting line. "You can take the left side, brother," said Steven as Drago got to the starting line. "I know it is your favorite." The dragons took their marks. Zigoto raised his hand. When his hand fell, the race would begin. As he watched the wise dragon's hand, Drago realized that his feet were stuck to the ground. Zigoto's dropped his hand. Steven took off into the air. Drago pushed and pushed as hard as he could. Finally, he lifted off into the air.

Already tired from the fight to get off the ground, Drago was in hot pursuit. Steven was well out in front. There seemed to be no way for Drago to catch his brother. The race stretched across the valley. Steven started to make significant long swirls through the air.

The older brother was already celebrating winning the dragon race. The shaking and waving through the air knocked loose the super glue from Steven's pocket. Steven tried to catch the tube. Glue squirted onto Steven's right-wing.

The beating of his wings caused Steven's wings to get stuck together. Drago was flapping his wings very hard. He was focused on winning the race and nothing else. When Drago reached the finish line, Emily came running up to him. "You won!" She yelled as she hugged Drago. Drago was so ex- cited to have won, but he wondered where his brother had gone. "Help!"

Steven yelled as he lay trapped. Steven had super glued himself to a tree.

Moral of the story

Cheaters never prosper.

Happy Martha!

On Princess Lane, there was a big, brown house that had no one living in it. The big, brown house had the largest yard on the street and a sign in the front yard that said 'For Sale.'

One day, a lady drove by and parked her car in front of the big, brown house. She got out of the car, walked over to the 'For Sale' sign, took it down, and replaced it with a 'Sold' sign. All the people who lived on Princess Lane looked out their windows, curious about who would be their new neighbors.

Next door to the big, brown house lived a little girl named Anna. Anna very much wanted a new little friend to move into the big, brown house and waited with much anticipation as she peeked from behind her window curtains. Anna continued to watch out the window until finally, a huge moving van pulled up in front of the house, and right behind the moving van was a car full of people.

Anna kept her eyes on the car, hoping her wishes would come true. The front doors of the car opened, and two tall adults got out. Anna was disappointed there was no little friend in the car. Then one of the adults opened the back door, and much to Anna's delight, a little girl, came rushing out!

Anna was pleased that her new neighbor was a little girl just her size, so Anna hurried over to her front door, opened it, and stood on her front porch to watch her new neighbor dance and sing around the yard. The new little girl stopped dancing and singing when she saw Anna standing on her front porch and excitedly ran toward Anna, coming to a halt right in front of her.

"Hello, my name is Martha. I am 5 years old. What is your name?" Martha asked. Anna smiled and responded, "My name is Anna, and I am also five years old. We are the same age!" Martha laughed and smiled. "I am your new neighbor. My giants and I are moving into our new house!" Anna looked at Martha. "Who are your giants?" Martha laughed and skipped around Anna and then pointed toward her house.

Her parents were standing on the front porch. "Those are my giants!" Martha yelled gleefully. "But that is you, Mommy and

Daddy," Anna replied. Martha continued to skip around Anna. "I know, but I call them my giants because they are so big!"

Martha grabbed Anna by her hands, and the two little girls started to dance and sing around the yard.

Anna stopped for a moment and said, "I think I will call you Happy Martha!" Martha looked at Anna and asked, "Why is that?" "Because you are cheerful, sunny, and merry!" Anna answered. "That's what 'Happy' means!"

Martha liked being called 'Happy Martha' and continued to skip and dance around Anna. As Martha was dancing, both little girls heard Anna's front door open. They looked toward Anna's house and saw three dogs racing out the front door. With their tails wagging, the dogs stopped in front of Anna, hoping for Anna to bend down and pat them on their heads. Martha looked at Anna and asked, "Are these your doggies?"

"Yes," Anna answered. "And inside my house, I also have three turtles, two cats, one canary, a rabbit, and many, many goldfish!"

Martha looked astonished. "I will call you Animal Anna!"

Martha and Anna both laughed at their new nicknames. They continued to dance and sing around the yard as the drivers loaded up Martha's house with all the furniture and toys.

Meanwhile, on the other side of Martha's house, a little boy stood there watching Martha and Anna from his front porch. He had a scowl on his face as he watched the two little girls dance and sing.

Martha saw the little boy and asked Anna, "Who is that?" Anna looked over and saw the little boy and answered, "That is Tommy. He is also five years old. He lives next to you on the other side. Tommy is a brat!" "Why do you say that, Animal Anna?" "Because all he wants to do is have a miserable time, and he is mean. I call him Terrible Tommy." "I will try to be friends with him," Martha said.

"Be careful, Happy Martha. Terrible Tommy doesn't like anyone!" Martha started to dance and sing again as she looked at Tommy, who stuck his tongue out at Martha and went back into his house. "I see what you mean, Animal Anna," Martha said as she wondered what was wrong with Tommy.

The next day, Anna came back over to Martha's house to see if Martha wanted to play. Martha told Anna she was unhappy Tommy ruined her party and couldn't understand what was wrong with him. "Animal Anna, what are we going to do about Terrible Tommy?" Martha asked.

"Happy Martha, I think Terrible Tommy is a lost cause. He ruined your party, and you should not talk to him." Martha sighed, "I don't like being unhappy. I think I will go over and talk to him." Anna just shrugged her shoulders and said, "Ok, but good luck." Martha ran out of her house and went straight over to Tommy's house. She knocked on the door, and Tommy opened it. "What do you want?" Tommy sneered.

"I want to be your friend, Tommy," Martha answered. Tommy looked at Martha and said, "Go away! I don't want any friends!" Tommy slammed the door shut, leaving Martha standing on the doorstep. Martha shook her head and walked back to her house, where Anna was waiting in the yard. "Well?" Anna asked.

Martha looked at Anna and said, "Animal Anna, there is something wrong with Terrible Tommy, but I just don't know what it is."

Every time Martha saw Tommy, she tried to be nice to him, but Tommy ignored her or had something mean to say. Then one day, Martha tried to talk to her parents about the problem with

41

Tommy. Still, her parents told her that Tommy was a bad influence on Martha and that Martha should stay away from him.

Martha was not happy with her parents and knew she had to talk to Anna about it. Martha went over to Anna's house and found her outside in her backyard playing with her dogs and cats. "Animal Anna, I have a problem," Martha began. Anna stopped playing with her pets and listened to Martha. "My giants told me that I couldn't be around Terrible Tommy anymore because he is mean.

What should I do, Animal Anna?" "Happy Martha, I think what Terrible Tommy needs is a lot of attention," Anna said. Martha looked over at Anna. "Animal Anna, I think you are right! But what kind of attention would make Terrible Tommy a nicer person?" Martha and Anna stood there and thought about the situation, but neither could develop any ideas to help Tommy.

Finally, Martha's Daddy yelled for Martha to come home for dinner. "Animal Anna, it sounds like I have to go home and have dinner with my giants. Let's try to think of something by tonight." "Ok, Happy Martha, but it isn't going to be easy."

As Martha sat at the dinner table, she overheard her Mommy say that Tommy's birthday was this weekend. His parents were unsure if they were going to have a birthday party for him. They were still mad at him for ruining Martha's party and wanted to teach him a lesson. Martha sat there for a moment until, all of a sudden, an idea came into her head.

Martha's idea was to throw Tommy a surprise birthday party! Martha told her parents about Tommy's need for attention. After a few minutes of talking, everyone agreed that a surprise birthday party would be a great idea. Martha's parents said they would speak to Tommy's parents and set it up. Martha was excited about her new idea and asked to be excused from the dinner table because she had a lot of planning to do.

Martha ran over to Anna's house and knocked on the door. When Anna opened the door, Martha told her the idea that she had. Anna also thought it was a great idea, and the two of them skipped and sang on Anna's front steps. Meanwhile, Tommy stared at Martha and Anna from his bedroom window, scowling at them but also wondering what they were up to.

With her parents' help, Tommy's parents and Anna, Martha, started to plan a surprise birthday party for Tommy. The whole week they organized the event and set a date for Saturday. Martha was in charge of inviting all her classmates and telling them not to tell Tommy. When Saturday arrived, Tommy sat on his front porch and watched all his little buddies from school arrive at Martha's house.

Every one of them carried a wrapped present in their hands as they walked up to the front door and entered. Tommy got mad that he was not invited to Martha's house and stood up, stomping his feet before returning to his home. Tommy stomped his feet over to the dining room table and sat down, putting his head on the table. Tommy's parents asked him why he was upset, but Tommy wouldn't answer them. As Tommy sat there pouting, the doorbell rang.

Tommy's parents said they were busy and asked Tommy to answer the door. Tommy got up and stomped his way to the front door, then reached for the doorknob to open it.

When Tommy opened the door, all his classmates were standing on his front porch with presents in their hands and at the same time yelled, "HAPPY BIRTHDAY, TOMMY!" Tommy just stood there and didn't know what to say. Martha, who was standing in front of the group, ran over to Tommy and gave him a big hug. "Are you surprised, Tommy?"

Martha cheerfully asked after she hugged him. Tommy felt a lump in his throat as he finally said, "Yes, but how did you know it was my birthday?" "My giants told me, so Animal Anna and I planned a surprise birthday party for you!" "Really? For me?" Tommy asked. Tommy's parents came to the front door and asked all the children to go in and sit in the living room. Martha's parents and Anna's came over and helped set up the decorations, along with the tables and chairs for everyone to sit.

All of Tommy's classmates put their birthday presents on one of the tables, and everyone laughed and smiled. Tommy started to feel strange about what was happening, and he realized that it was a good feeling. He found himself laughing and talking with everyone and could not believe they were nice enough to have a party for him.

Feeling a little embarrassed, Tommy went over to Martha. He said, "Martha, I am sorry I ruined your 'Welcome to the Neighborhood' party a few weeks ago."

Martha smiled and patted Tommy on the shoulder. "That is ok, Tommy. I forgive you, and from now on, I will never call you Terrible Tommy again!" Tommy smiled back at Martha when she said that, thinking to himself that his new little neighbor was a nice person.

Tommy also realized that being superior to others makes them feel happy and cheerful, so Tommy decided from now on he would be a good friend to Martha, Anna, and all his

Helping Dad Paint

It was along about the first week of spring that William's father said to his mother, "I guess I will paint the family room this week." William heard this and ran over to his father and said, "Can I help, please?" His father looked over to William's mother with a smile and said, "What do you think?" She looked at him then at William and said, "If you be careful, I think you can help." William jumped up and down and ran to his room. He opened his closet and looked around.

When his mother came into his room, she saw William in the closet. She said, "What are you looking for, William?" without turning around, William breathlessly said, "I'm looking for my painting clothes." His mother laughed and said, "You don't have any, but I am sure I can find something for you." After William's mother looked, she found a pair of old pants that are getting too short for him and a shirt with a rip on the sleeve. William put them over his desk chair to be ready for when he wants to wear them. The next week William's father put some sheets over the family room furniture and covered the floor.

William got into the clothes his mother gave him and rushed out to the family room. "Are we going to start now?" he asked his father. "Yes, William." He answered, "And be careful, ok?" "I will, daddy." Said William. William's father opened a can of paint and poured some into the tray on the floor. He gave William a paintbrush and showed him how to dip it into the paint. Then he said, "Now William, I want you to paint like this over here on this wall." And he pointed the wall out to William. "Ok, daddy." William brushed the paint onto the wall just like his father had shown him. He brushed up and then down up and down until there was no more paint on the brush. "All done." He said. Then he said, "This is no fun." He put the meeting down and went outside to play, saying, "Thanks, daddy." And with that, William's painting day was over.

Making Friends

One day William was playing in the yard, and his mother came out to see what he was doing. She said, "William, let's go to the park, and you can play on the swings while I read my book there. It's such a nice day." William looked up at her and said, "Ok, but can I take my cowboy hat with?" his mother said, "Sure. Let's go." So, William and his mother locked up the house and walked to the park about a block away. When they got there, William went over to the swings and said to his mother, "Mom, give me a push on the swing." So, William's mother helped him on then gave him a push to start him off.

William learned how to keep himself going, so his mother went over to the nearby bench and sat down to read her book. William swung up and back and soon was getting tired of the swing. Along with then, another mother came by with her son too. He was about Williams's age and size and looked at William when he came near. "Hello." The woman said to William's mother. "Hello." Said William's mother to the other mother. "And who do we have here?" she asked. "This is Johnny." Said the other mother.

"He is five." She continued. "I am five and a half." Said Johnny. His mother rolled her eyes and said, "My mistake, five and one half." She laughed. "What is your son's name?" she said. "This is

William. He is the same age as your Johnny." Said William's mother. "Say hello, William." She said. William stopped the swing and went over to Johnny and said, "Hello. Do you want to play cowboys?" Johnny looked at his mother, and she nodded yes. "Ok." Said Johnny. The two boys went off ways into the grass. "Don't go too far." Said Johnny's mother. "We won't," they both said to her, and then they sat down on the ground.

Johnny's mother and William's mother sat together and talked about the boys as the two boys played in the grass. "Why don't you be Billy the Kid, and I can be the sheriff." Said William. Johnny said, "Ok, but I get to ride off on my horse."
"Sure thing." Said William. The two of them played the whole afternoon until William's mother said to him, "Time to go home, William." "Mom, do we have to?" he said. "Yes, I have to start

dinner for us." She said. William turned to Johnny and said, "I have to go now, but we can be friends, can't we?" Johnny looked at William and said, "I guess so. Maybe we can come to the park again sometime, and then I can be the sheriff." So, William and his mother said goodbye to their new friends and started walking home.

Playing Pirate

Summertime is an excellent time for William. He likes to play in the backyard, one time a cowboy, then another a soldier. One night his mother read him a story about pirates. William liked it very much, and the next morning, he made his mom make an eye patch to put over his eye and got an old hat that his father didn't use anymore, then ran out back into the yard. William ran back and forth, yelling like a pirate in the storybook his mom had read the night before. He soon tired of running then remembered that the book's pirate looked for buried treasure on an island.

He went back into the house and into his room, where he took a paper and drew a map. Right in the middle, he put a big X to mark the spot where the gold was buried. William looked at what he had drawn and nodded. "That should do." And with that, he ran back outside. William looked around and found a tree branch about just the right size to use as a sword. Then he walked over to the big tree at the back of the yard and stood under it for a while. He sat down and took out the map he drew and studied it. "If I start here under this tree and walk this way till I come to that the stone over there, I should find the treasure." So, he got up and walked over to the stone.

He looked at the map again then walked over to the trash cans. William turned around then walked to the center of the yard. "This is the spot where the X shows on my map." He said. He bent down and looked real hard at the ground, but there wasn't anything to see there. William's mother watched him from the kitchen window, and she saw him bending down in the center of the yard. When she saw William come back into the house, she asked him what he was doing. "I'm looking for buried treasure, mom, but I have to fix my map." So, William ran back to his room to draw a better map. William's mother had an idea, and she went out to the yard and placed something in the center of the where William was looking before.

She rushed back into the kitchen before William came out of his room. "Is your map ok now?" she asked him. "I think so." Said

William. "Why don't you try again? Maybe this time your map is right." She said, smiling a little. "I will." Said William as he went back into the yard. He ran to the tree again, then to the stone, then to the cans, and finally to the center and the X on his map.

William got down on his hands and knees and looked real hard at the grass. All of a sudden, his eyes lit up, and he spotted something shiny in the grass. He picked it up. It was a quarter. "Wow!" ex- claimed William. He ran into the house and showed the coin to his mother. "Look at the treasure I found." He said to her. "I told you that there was a treasure out there." "That's great, William." And then William went back out to the yard to look for more treasure. His mother gave a short laugh and went on cleaning the kitchen.

The Empty Box

John Bixby turned ten on Sunday. He liked to play ball in his home's back yard because it had no trees as yet since the family just moved in last month. The neighborhood was old, but the house his parents were renting was newly remodeled on a vacant lot. John was playing there, hitting the ball and then running after it to hit it again. His mom and dad were going to the store to buy some food. They had very little because John's father had been out of work for so long and just got a job. John was old enough to be alone, and they made him promise that he would not leave the yard.

John hit the ball, and it flew to the end of the yard; there were the neighbor's shrubs in the back. John went into the bushes to find his ball. He looked everywhere, but the ball just seemed to have vanished. John was just about to give up when his foot tapped something buried in the ground under the bushes. He bent down and brushed away some of the dirt. Just under the surface, he saw what looked like a small box, old and dirty, peeking out from under the bush. John dug with his shoe and pulled the box out from its hiding place.

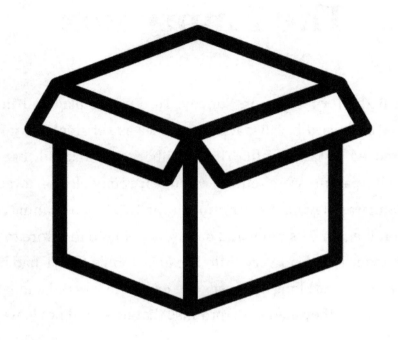

There were no markings John could see on the box, just streaks of dirt. He sat down right there under the bushes and tried to open it. It was tightly fitted, and he had to pry one side then the other with his small pocket knife until the lid finally came off. John looked in and saw that the box was empty. "Why would anybody bury an empty box?" John thought to himself. He was just about to toss it back on the ground, and as he moved his hand back, the box made a noise like something sliding. John opened it again and looked at it a little better this time. The outside bottom of the box looked to be longer than the inside. "That's strange," said John to himself. He reached in and tapped the bottom. It sounded hollow. Now John was curious and ran his finger along the inside bottom of the box. There, on one side, he felt a little tab or something. He gripped it with his fingertips and tugged at it. As the false bottom came away, John saw a piece of paper on the box's real bottom. He grabbed and unfolded it. That paper was some sort of map.

John couldn't make any sense of it. There were funny markings and lines drawn all over it. John looked into the now empty box again to make sure that it was real and tossed the box to the side. There was a date on the map, 1941. "Wow!" ex- claimed John. "That was a long time ago." he thought to himself. He took the map, and as he was going back to his yard, he spotted his ball and picked it up as he got out again. He ran to his room and sat on his bed, looking at the map he had found.

"What does it all mean?" he said. The map had lines here and there with small crosses and one large one off to the right. There were no names on the map but just three letters with numbers after them. The letters were H and R, and numbers after them. John could not make heads or tails of it. He set the map down on his nightstand. I guess I will have to think about it some more later. John liked to play baseball, and his favorite team was just about to play, so he turned on his TV and propped up his pillow to watch the game. After the first few innings, John watched the game, one of his team's batters came to the plate.

On the TV screen on the bottom-up popped three letters John had seen earlier in the day. H, R, and E. "Hits runs and errors!" shouted John. John grabbed the map again and looked at the letters on the map. There it was, H 2213, R 2174 for R, H 3415,

R 1736 for W. What was the meaning of the R and W? John could not figure it out. As he looked at the map again, John turned it left then right. It still made no sense to him. Then he turned it upside-down. Furthermore, he couldn't figure it out.

John laid his head down and held the map up. Still, nothing came to mind. Feeling frustrated, John heard the announcer on the TV say something and looked at it to see what was going on. The map in his hand hung down over his fingers, and now when John looked at the map again, he could see through the backside, and the light from the window made it clear so he could see the map on the front.

The jumble of letters that were backward on the front was now readable to him. It said, "Start at the corner of the shed." And an X was there. "What shed?" thought John. He got up, went back to the bushes, and pushed through to the backyard next door. In the corner, John looked around, and there was an old shed with the doors coming off and the wood so old that it was grey. The shed looked to John to be hundreds of years old and was falling apart. John walked over to the hut and stood at the corner as it was shown on the map. It started to make sense to him now that he had a starting point.

He followed the instructions as best he could until he got to the last big X. It brought him to his yard to an old tree just on edge. It was the only tree on their property and was left there because it was out of the way and looked still in good shape. John walked around the tree, looking at it closely.

There was no sign of anything out of the ordinary as far as he could make out. John folded the map and put it in his back pocket. The only thing left was to climb the tree. John grabbed a low limb and started to climb up. The higher he got, the more John looked down.

He was up about twenty feet when he looked up and saw a small slit. John stopped and looked closer at the cut in the tree. It looked like someone had made a hole at one time, but the tree was healing itself, and the gap had closed up and was almost gone. John pulled out his pocket knife and tried to make the hole a little bigger. It took him just a few minutes, but he could get it open enough to see that there was a hollow behind the small hole. Inside he spotted what looked like another piece of paper folded in half twice. It looked ancient, but the tree hollow had kept it dry.

John slid two fingers into the slit and was just able to touch the paper. It was too far in for him to get a good hold on it, so he reached up and pulled a tiny twig off the tree and used it with his knife to wiggle the paper out. When John got it out, he saw that the paper was wrapped around something. He slowly opened the paper. There inside the paper were two baseball cards. To his amazement, they were for Babe Ruth, and the other was for Honus Wagner.

Now John, being a big-time baseball fan, knew the names of these two very well and was happy that he had figured out the map. Those markings, H for hits and R for runs, now made more sense, and the R and H stood for Ruth and Wagner now were understood as well. He climbed down, and when his dad and mom came home, he told them all about the map and what he had found. His dad was beside himself.

He sat down and started to cry. John came to him and asked his dad what's wrong. He said to John, "John, these two cards are worth a fortune." "We can now have a so much better life because of what you have found." John looked at his father and smiled.

William and the Circus

When William was five, his mother wanted to give him a lovely birthday present. She thought and thought but couldn't think of anything that he would like. She talked to William's father, but he didn't know anything either. When the Sunday paper came, William's mother read about the circus coming to town and would be starting the next Saturday. She asked William's father what he thought, and he agreed that it was a good idea, so William's mother went to the store where tickets were being sold for the circus.

She bought three for her, her husband, and William. She didn't tell him that they were going. When Saturday came, and William's mother woke him up, she said to him, "I have a surprise for you for your birthday. You have been so good that your father and I are taking you to the circus today." All William could say was, "Hooray." Then William ran around the room jumping up and down.

He went into his bedroom and opened his toy box. Out came the toy lion and then the bear. William had a whole set of toy animals. Then he took out two clowns that were also in the toy box. He played with it until he thought to himself, "When are we going?" he ran to his mother and asked her. She said to him, "We will be going later this afternoon." William could hardly wait. The day seemed to go by so slowly that William kept asking his mother when? He ate some lunch, and his mom said that he should take a nap. He laid down on his bed with the toy tiger and bear.

"I'm not sleepy." Said William. But after a while, he closed his eyes and was asleep and dreaming of the circus. A little later, when his mother came into his room, she woke William up and put out some clothes to change. William got up and changed clothes, then came out to the kitchen where his mother and father were. "Are we going now?" asked William. "Yes." Said his mother, and the three of them went out and got into the car. The drive to the circus was only a short time, but it was forever to William.

As they rounded a corner, William saw the big tent with little ones around it ahead of them. "Wow, mom, look at that." He said to his mother. William's father parked the car, and the three of them walked over to the big tent and got in line. William was so excited he kept trying to look around the people in front of them. "I can't see." He said to his mother. "Be patient, William." His mother said. When they entered the tent, William's eyes lit up. There were lots of people already there. They found some seats near the center of the chairs, and William sat between his parents.

Soon all were seated, and the music started. Into the tent came a parade of people and animals. "Look, mom, elephants." Said William. The show went on for over two hours. There were jugglers, acrobats, clowns, and animals. When the lion show started, William sat close to his father. They were so much bigger than he thought they would be. In the end, there was another parade, and then it was all over. William and his mother and father left the tent and drove home.

William talked about the circus and that he wanted to join one when he grew up. His mother smiled, thinking of all the other times William had said what he wanted to be when he got bigger. One time a policeman than a fireman now working in a circus. When they got home, it was very late, so William said good night to his parents, and his mom put him in bed. "That's what I want to be when I get big." He said once again as his mother closed the door partway as usual. She thought to herself as she walked out,

"There is still a lot of time before that will happen, William. Take your time growing up."

William Meets a Beggar

In the early spring, William and his mom went to the town square to shop for some summer clothes. They went in one store after another, and soon William was getting tired. "This is boring." He said to his mom. "I know it is for you. Why don't we stop for some ice cream? Ok?" Said his mom. Now William will be five soon, so this was a treat for him. "Hooray!" said William, and he was happy to get some ice cream. They walked into a few more stores until William said, "Now, mom?" And his mother said, "All right. It's across the street."

And she leads him across to the ice cream store. As they went in William, saw a man dressed in a uniform, and he had no legs. There was a cup there, and William's mom put a dollar in it. William looked back, and he heard the man say, "God bless and thank you." To his mother. William was a little scared and hid behind his mom's dress as they stood at the counter. When his mom gave him the ice cream, he looked at it and ate it slowly as he watched the man outside. When they were finished, they walked out again, but now the man was gone.

When they got home, William thought about the man and went to his mom. "Mommy." He said. "Yes, dear?" She answered. "Why didn't that man have any legs?" His mother thought a while then said, "Oh, you mean the man by the ice cream store. Well, it looks like he lost them in the Army fighting to keep us safe." "He scared me a little." Said William." "Don't be afraid.

He did something right, and we should be proud of him. Your father was in the Army too, and we were lucky that he came home with both of his legs." That night William included the man in his prayers. His mom was so happy to hear it that she started to cry a little. William was growing up so fast, she thought to herself. William thought about that man all week. He felt terrible for him, and he wanted to do something. When his mom said that they were going to town again, William asked if they would get ice cream. His mom said, "I guess so if you behave."

So, when they were finished shopping William, and his mom went to the ice cream shop, and as they got there, the soldier without legs was there again. His mother also gave him a dollar, and they went in and ordered ice cream. William's mom gave him a cone. Then he did something different. He walked outside and gave it to the man out. William stepped back and gave a salute as he saw in the movies, and the man laughed and saluted back. William's mom saw what he had done and bought another cone for him. As they left, William turned and waved at the man who waved back and said as they walked by, "God bless and thank you."

Building a life

Kindness

Doing something kind and generous for someone else often takes effort, and yet each time you do it, you realize that it's the best way to live.

Look for ways to make someone else's day or week a little brighter, a little more enjoyable, a little more relaxing, a bit of fun. As you do, you're making your day or week the same.

Forgiveness

Choosing to forgive another is one of the hardest things most people ever do, especially if it's undeserved. It's hard because it's not human nature. Human nature cries out for revenge and retribution. But why get stuck in human nature? Whether that person who wronged you deserves forgiveness or not is not the central issue. The central point is you are doing the right thing. Forgiveness is more significant than justice. Justice is human; forgiveness is divine.

Tolerance

It's easy to respect people with who you have a lot in common, but respecting others' right to think and be different is even more critical, as well as more endearing.

Gratitude

Gratitude causes us to focus on all the beautiful things we have instead of what we think we're missing or haven't yet received. Recognizing that we have so much, and focusing with gratitude on that abundance, opens the door for more blessings to come into our lives.

Faith

Faith is believing, faith is hoping, faith is trusting. Faith refuses to call anything impossible. Faith refuses to quit or to be defeated. Faith refuses to allow its joy and peace to be stolen by circumstances or difficulties.

Desire to Learn

Look at the little birds as they learn how to take flight for the first time. Look at the little kittens and puppies and how enthusiastic they are about each opportunity to explore and learn new things. Learning and growing make the world beautiful, and it can make your life beautiful as well.

Perseverance

A little more persistence, a bit more effort, and what seemed hopeless failure may turn into glorious success. When you're not good at something, you encounter a lot of seeming "failure." But if you keep doing it over and over, and learning from the reactions you get, pretty soon, you'll be good and then great.

Courage

A new challenge can be very awkward, even scary at first. But suppose we deliberately put ourselves out there and do the very thing that we're afraid of. In that case, it becomes more comfortable, and we get better at it. Eventually, we will no longer be afraid. That is conquering our fears!

Positive Attitude

It's only natural to see all the things that are wrong with the situation, remember all the times you had it better, or look at those who currently seem to have it better. Still, you're not going to be happy that way. You will be satisfied, though, if you decide that you're going to be thankful for what you have, rather than dwelling on what you don't have.

Generosity

If we give to others, yield to their wishes to make them happy, or put their needs above our own, we can sometimes feel like we're losing out. But we're not really. God sees such unselfishness, and He will reward it. You never lose by giving.

Respect

Respect is manifested through consideration, understanding, thoughtfulness, a willingness to listen, and loving communication. And it works both ways; if you want people to show you respect, show them respect.

Patience

Patience is the ability to persevere when faced with difficulties. We often need to be patient, either with people or with circumstances, and we need to do so in a spirit of love.

Anger management

Genuinely great folks never stoop to answer petty things; The unkind word, the bitter cut, rankles deep and stings. They are too big to notice them. They simply pass them by, And even with a smile sometimes or twinkle in the eye. For they have found that after all 'twas better, in the end, to meet it with a smile, and then, just let it pass, my friend.

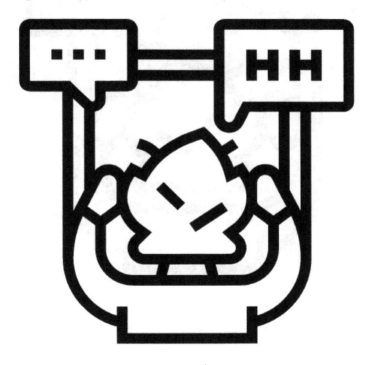

Personal Responsibility

We have the capability of making independent choices. We are personally responsible for our decisions and their outcomes. We must take responsibility for how things play out.

The Other Side of the Fence

Cheeps is a little chick that loves to learn about new things, just like you! He is always looking for adventures on the farm. He loves living there but what Cheeps wants is to cross the fence surrounding the farm and explore the world.

Cheeps has lots of fun with his best friend, Chuck. Sometimes, Chuck is unsure about Cheeps' ideas, like the day he tried to fly hanging from a kite and landed on a cow's back! Or the day he fed the pigs with "mud and worm pie" because he thought it was delicious. Even though Cheeps' has some crazy ideas, Chuck still loves his friend. "Come on, Chuck, imagine all the things we could discover on the other side of the fence," says Cheeps.

"I don't know, Cheeps, our parents told us to stay away from it. There are foxes out there. What if a fox decides we are his next dinner?" asks Chuck with a frightened face. "You don't have to worry about foxes, Chuck, and I'm sure they would prefer to eat rabbits over chicks. They are the juiciest," smiled Cheeps. "If you say so," said Chuck. That night when Cheeps went to bed, he couldn't sleep.

He imagined how it would be out there. He knew there was a river near the farm. The grown-up chicks often talked about it. Cheeps wanted to go to the river to swim and dive in the freshwater.

"I know I'll be a great swimmer," he thought. But what could they do to cross the fence? Cheeps was trying to figure it out. First, Cheeps thought to jump the wall. Then he realized it was too high for them.

Next, he thought to make a hole in the wooden fence, but he would need a saw. "Too dangerous! Not a good idea," Cheeps said out loud. Finally, he had a great idea! They will dig under the fence to cross to the other side.

Tomorrow is the day! Chuck and I will go to the other side, and we will have lots of fun at the river," he said to himself. The next day Cheeps and Chuck waited until the other chickens gathered to eat. Then when nobody was around, they started to dig. "Hurry up, Chuck, we need to dig fast before the others look for us," said Cheeps. "I ate too many worms this morning! My belly is getting in the way," laughed Chuck. "Are you sure this is a good idea?"

"It is. Don't be such a chicken," said Cheeps. "But I am a chicken!" said Chuck proudly. We are almost there, Chuck", said Cheeps. "I see something! Just here, it's black", said Chuck. "And it feels wet. Do you see it, Cheeps?" Cheeps didn't answer. "Cheeps, are you there? Cheeps?" Chuck was almost on the other side. His belly was stuck be- tween the fence and the ground.

He pushed himself hard one time, two times... and PLOP! He rolled and bumped into something. He made it through. His head was spinning. Chuck looked around, but he didn't see Cheeps anywhere.

"Where is Cheeps?" whispered Chuck. "This is so strange. He would never leave me here alone." "Cheeeeps, where are you?" he yelled. "Stop playing pranks on me. It is not funny." Just at that moment, Chuck heard a mumbling sound. He lifted his head, and he couldn't believe what he was looking at. It was a fox! There was Cheeps, right in the fox's mouth!

"Oh no, I knew this was another crazy idea, Cheeps!" Chuck exclaimed, walking backward. "What am I going to do? This fox is going to eat both of us!" Chuck ran and hid behind a tree. "I need to go back to the farm," he thought. "But I can't leave Cheeps here. He is my best friend, and I know he would do the same for me.

Friends take care and help each other." Chuck was afraid, but he was determined to save Cheeps from the fox. "If that fox doesn't eat us both, I'm going to lock Cheeps in the chicken coop and leave him there forever!" mumbled Chuck. Chuck took a look. The fox was walking to the other side of the meadow carrying Cheeps in his mouth.

"Hey you, furball. Come here!" yelled Chuck. "Do you want to eat that rotten chick? I am tastier than him. Come and get me if you can!" Chuck ran as fast as he could towards the fence. The fox chased after him. Chuck was a very slow chick. The fox got closer and closer. He was soon near enough to grab Chuck.

He opened his mouth, and Cheeps hit the ground. He was covered in drool, but he was safe. Chuck hurried and got into the same hole he dug before. The fox ran so fast that he couldn't stop and hit his head on the fence post. It knocked him silly! "Quick Cheeps, run before the fox wakes up and tries to eat us again," yelled Chuck.

"Phewww, that was close!" said Cheeps. "Rotten chick? Really?" "It was the first idea that popped into my head," laughed Chuck. "After all, I think you were right, Chuck, it was not a good idea. I'll listen to you next time. Thanks for saving me," said Cheeps as he hugged Chuck. "It's ok, that's what friends are for!" said Chuck. "Just promise me our next adventure will be here on the farm."

"Now I'm more afraid about what our parents are going to say! That makes the fox seem not so scary," said Cheeps. They both laughed and walked home.

Lenny the Lion

Lenny the Lion Wants a Fish

Lenny quietly tiptoed away from his pride. The light of day was beginning to show, and before long, the sun would rise above the mountains. Lenny wanted to play down by the river, and he knew his parents would never let him do that by himself. He wanted to show them that he was old enough and smart enough and strong enough to take care of himself.

As soon as he was away from the other lions, Lenny ran toward the river. He had been watching other lions catch and eat fish from that river, and it looked like fun. It also looked like an excellent way to get so much to eat that he would not have to share, like when his mother caught the fish or other food. Then all the young lions would have to share what there was and eat what they could. No one ever got enough that way.

But today, Lenny was going to fill his stomach so much he would not have to eat the rest of the day again. Lenny decided he had chosen a good day to catch fish, so he slowly stood up and crept up to the edge of the river. He was still careful like his mother had taught him so that he did not get surprised and hurt by other animals that wanted to eat him. Lenny stopped at the edge of the river.

He bent over and lapped up some water. It was cool and yummy to the taste. He jumped when he heard something moving in the bushes nearby, but then he settled down as he saw a snake slither away with a frog in his mouth. Lenny was beginning to become afraid. He wanted to hunt and fish like an adult lion and catch his food. But he was also scared that he might get hurt and there would be no one from his pride to come and rescue him. Lenny watched the river again. Now he saw something moving in the water. It looked like a big log, but it was slowly moving toward him.

He bent to drink some more water be- fore wading into the river to catch some fish. Suddenly, the log in the river leaped toward him. The record opened its mouth and hissed at him, showing big teeth. Lenny knew right away... it was a crocodile! And it wanted to eat Lenny for its meal. Lenny quickly ran for his life away from the river. He heard the clomping of the crocodile's big feet in the grass, and he heard it snap its big jaws, trying to catch Lenny.

But Lenny kept running and did not stop until he was back with his pride again. He ran up to his mother, who was sitting in the sun, grooming his brothers and sisters. Mother stopped when she saw Lenny running up to her. "Where have you been?" she asked. "I was afraid you might have gone to the river, even though we told you it is dangerous."

Lenny ran over the top of his mother and hid behind her, looking back toward the river. Still trying to catch his breath, he said, "I went to the river so that I could catch a fish for my meal.

It looked safe enough, but a giant crocodile jumped out of the water and tried to eat me. I ran and ran back here. I should have listened to you and Father.

I promise never to do that again." "It would have been better if you had listened to me and believed I have enough experience to know how to protect you," Mother said. "But I'm glad you returned safely. We'll all go down to the river later to catch some fish for supper. It's safer when we are all together."

Lenny and the Wildebeest

Lenny strayed away from his pride. He wanted to practice his hunting skills by sneaking up on a smaller animal, then pouncing on it. He didn't want to eat it, and he just wanted to practice pouncing. He walked slowly and silently through the tall grass. He listened carefully to the sound of the wind in the grass, to the chirping of the grasshoppers and the croaking of the frogs.

Lenny heard something he could not describe. It sounded like an animal grunting and groaning. Then it would stop for a while and start up again after a few minutes. Lenny crept in the direction of those sounds to find out what it was. When he came to the edge of the tall grass, he stopped and listened and waited. He also sniffed the air to help him find out what was making the grunting noises. Between the edge of the tall grass and the edge of the river was a large mud puddle.

In the middle of the mud puddle was a wildebeest. It was bigger than Lenny's mother and father. It was stuck in the mud puddle. While Lenny was watching, the wildebeest started struggling again, trying to get out of the reservoir. But it was stuck. Lenny walked up to the wildebeest to get a closer look. When the wildebeest smelled a lion, he was afraid and struggled even more challenging to get free.

But when he saw little Lenny, he stopped working to catch his breath. "How long have you been caught in the mud?" Lenny asked the wildebeest. The wildebeest panted and snorted to catch its breath after all the struggling. "I have been here since the early morning sun," said the wildebeest.

Lenny had never seen a wildebeest up close before. He knew the older lions hunted and chased them, but he had never spoken to one of them. "Where is your family?" he asked. "They were afraid of getting caught by lions, so they ran away when I got stuck here." "How can you get out of the mud?" Lenny asked. He didn't know mud could be deep and dangerous. The wildebeest blew out a full breath. "I don't know. I have very little strength left to try to climb out," he said.

Lenny looked around the area. He saw a dead tree leaning over the mud puddle and wondered if it might help the stuck wildebeest. He pointed his nose at the tree, then looked back at the wildebeest. "If I can knock that tree into the mud, would it help you climb out?" he asked. "Yes, it might help me.

But why would you want to help me?" asked the confused and tired wildebeest. "I'm too small to chase after you," Lenny said. "It's no fun chasing something when you know it's too weak to get away. If I help you get free today, maybe you'll be stronger, and I can chase you tomorrow." The wildebeest laughed at the childish idea. But he wanted to get free, so he said, "If you can help me get free today, then I will help you if you ever need a friend when you get stuck," he said.

Lenny smiled. That sounds good," he said. So, Lenny climbed up the dead tree. It was scary because he was afraid the tree would break and make him fall into the mud beside the wildebeest. He carefully bounced on the tree until it broke, then he quickly jumped away from the ground and watched the stuck wildebeest.

The tree fell right in front of the tired wildebeest. It grabbed the tree limbs with his front hooves and slowly climbed out of the mud. Then it turned to look at Lenny. "Thank you, young lion. Do you promise not to chase me today?" he asked. Lenny silently nodded his head, and the muddy wildebeest quickly ran away before any other dangers could fall upon him.

The Rude Hyenas

One day, Lenny was out playing with three of his brothers and some of the hyena pups. They were wrestling in the grass and chasing each other around large boulders and having a good time.

After a while, Lenny's mother called her cubs to come back home. All three of Lenny's brothers immediately ran to their den to find out what their mother wanted. Lenny didn't want to stop playing, so he stayed with the hyena pups.

Once the other lion cubs were gone, the hyenas started playing rough with Lenny and ganging up on him in their rough play. One of the pups bit Lenny too hard on the back leg, and it hurt. But when Lenny started to complain to the puppies, they laughed and told him to go back to his mama as the other cubs did.

Lenny didn't understand why they treated him that way and wondered whether he had done something wrong so that they made fun of him and hurt him as they did. But they just called him names and chased him some more—not as part of any game, but to try to hurt him again.

Lenny ran back to his brothers and his pride and left the hyenas to themselves. If they were going to hurt him, then he didn't want to play with them anyway. As soon as he saw his pride, he ran to them and told them what had happened.

Why did we have fun together, but as soon as I was alone with the hyenas, they started treating me differently and making fun of me? he asked his mother.

"Whenever you play with your brothers, you play rough without wanting to hurt each other because you are from the same family," she said. "But when you play with young ones from other animal families, they do not love you as much as we do, so they sometimes make fun of you and may even try to hurt you." "But why?" Lenny asked.

"I didn't do anything bad to them," he said. He wanted to understand why they treated him that way. Mother put her large paw on his shoulder and licked his ears to make him feel better. Then she looked at the wound on his back leg. "It will heal in a few days," she said softly. "If you want to be treated fairly, then it's better for you to stay with those who love you and will protect you from hunters and other animals.

But if you want to go out and meet other animals and play with them, you must understand that they don't love you the way we do and they may sometimes make fun of you. It is wrong, but it is also the way of the jungle." "Can I try to make it better, so we can all get along with each other?" he asked. Mother stopped licking his ears.

He was all better, now. "Yes, dear. I want you to make the world better, but you need to understand how it is and why it is first. Watch the other animals and try to be good with them. But don't expect them always to be good to you until they believe you are trying to do better first. Learn to love them, and they may learn to love you. Treat others how you want to be treated," she said.

Lenny and the Tortoise

Lenny liked to go out and make new friends. But he didn't like it when other animals ran away from him when he tried to play. Lenny walked into the jungle and saw a group of monkeys. They were happily swinging from the trees and chasing each other. It looked like good fun, so Lenny tried to join them. As soon as they saw him coming, they all started chattering and screaming and running to the tops of the trees for safety. They were afraid of the lion. Lenny was confused and hurt.

He looked up at the monkeys and said, "I want to play with you. Come down so we can play together." "No! No! Go away," they cried. We don't want to play with you." Then they started throwing things at Lenny to make him go away. Lenny slowly walked away from the monkeys. All he wanted to do was play with them. Why wouldn't they let him play? He wondered.

Next, Lenny walked into the grasslands. There, he saw a small herd of gazelle chasing and playing with each other. They were leaping high into the air and bouncing as they ran. Lenny smiled. Indeed, they will let him join their play. He ran over to them, but before he could talk to them, they saw him and ran away. Lenny called after them. Please let me play with you," he called. "I just want to play."

One of the younger gazelle turned around and looked at Lenny. "We don't want to play with you," she said. "Go away and leave us alone." Lenny sadly hung his head and frowned. He could not understand why the other animals would not play with him. He had no one else to play with and wanted a new friend. Lenny decided to go down by the river and see if any of the animals drinking water would like to be his friend. On the way, he walked through the jungle, and he walked through the tall grasslands.

He walked over the rocks and finally saw the river ahead of him. When Lenny looked down at the moving grass in front of him, he saw a tortoise. It was moving slowly toward the river. Lenny stopped and sniffed at the tortoise. Instantly, the tortoise crawled up inside his shell to protect himself. "Hello," Lenny called to Tortoise. "Anybody home?" He knew that was a stupid thing to say, but he didn't know what else to say. The tortoise slowly peeked out of his shell. "Ye-es," Tortoise said slowly.

He saw Lenny standing in his path and was afraid to come out of his body. Lenny lay down in front of Tortoise with his nose just inches away from the tortoiseshell opening. "Hi," said Lenny with a smile. "I'm looking for someone to play with. Will you play with me?"

"I am too slow to play with you," said Tortoise. "If you want a friend to play with, you should find someone the same size, with the same strength and speed as you." Lenny smiled. "That means I should play with my brothers," he said.

"If you play nice with your brothers, they will play nice with you," said Tortoise. "Then you will never have to search for friends, and you will never be bored or lonely." "Good idea. Thank you, Tortoise, for helping me to see that my best friends are my very own brothers."

Lenny Just Wants Breakfast

Lenny's mother nuzzled him with her nose. "It's time to get up, she said. He was still tired, and the spot he was lying on was warm, so he rolled over and went back to sleep. Later, Lenny woke up, stretched, and yawned real big. He was ready to get up, and the day was beginning to get warmer. He slowly walked over to his mother. "I'm hungry," Lenny said. "Where's breakfast?"

His mother smiled sadly. "I'm sorry, dear. The food is all gone. You wanted to sleep, and so your brothers ate all the food." Lenny looked around at a few bones on the ground. "What am I going to do?" he asked. "You'll have to wait until we get more food," she replied. "And next time, get out of bed when I tell you it's time to get up." Lenny's stomach started to grumble. It was empty, and he didn't know when he might eat again. So, he decided to find his food.

Lenny walked into the high grass, sniffing for something to eat. Suddenly, he heard quick movement and chased after the sounds. He saw a rabbit running away from him through the grass, and he started running after it, but the rabbit was too fast, so Lenny quit. Lenny walked onto some bare ground with a lot of holes all around. He didn't see any animals, but he waited patiently. Finally, several prairie dogs came out of the holes and started looking around.

Lenny jumped up and tried to grab one of them, but they also were too fast for him. Lenny was using all of his energy to find food, and he was getting real tired quickly. He took a deep breath and decided to return home without eating. He hoped there was going to be some food for him for supper. When he got home, he waited and waited for either his father or mother to bring back some food for their children. Finally, both his parents returned, but neither of them had any food.

"What will we eat tonight," the cubs all asked at the same time. Father sadly hung his head, knowing his children would cry without food to eat. "I'm sorry," he apologized. "Maybe the hunting will be better tomorrow. I will get up early and go see what I can find." So, Lenny went to bed with an empty stomach. He did not sleep well because he tossed and turned and dreamed about food. In the morning, when Lenny's mother woke up her children, she said, "Boys, it's time for breakfast."

Lenny instantly jumped out of bed and ran to where his father was standing. He had brought food back for the entire family. Lenny looked up at his mother. "I am sorry I didn't listen to you yesterday when you told me to get up to eat. I promise to listen to you from now on," he said. Lenny's mother smiled and licked his ears to let him know that she loved him.

Bright Star

Once upon a time, a cluster of stars lived high in the sky. At night it looked like millions of tiny flickering lights. All of the cluster family stars huddled up close to light up the sky. it was their job, and a significant one! Together they felt more substantial and brighter. Little Star was the youngest. She was different from the others. Although she had five pointy arms, she looked different. She was smaller and had one arm that was a little bit wonky – it often flopped up and down, especially during the huddling! Little Star had a dream, and she always imagined how she would travel higher up into the sky.

But the others would say, "You are not bright enough, Little Star – you belong here in the cluster." It made Little Star sad. In her heart, she knew there was more out there, and she wanted to find it! Every night just before the huddling started, Little Star would quietly sing to herself. It often made her feel better inside.

Sing! (To the tune of 'London Bridge's falling')

Shining bright that's what I do, in the sky, way up high Shining bright that's what I do No matter what they say!

One day Little Star felt annoyed with the others telling her that she wasn't bright enough. Brother Blue Star was very mean and kept on bumping into her, saying, "Who do you think you are, Little Star? – you will never be bright enough to make it any higher". She could hear the cluster family laughing at her. She felt sad and angry. She cried and cried until there were no more tears. Poor Little Star.

The next day Little Star woke up feeling more robust. She had a plan! "I will travel higher - up to the dream clouds. I'll visit the Twinklers!" The Twinklers were stars that didn't need each other to shine. They did it all by themselves. "I will be a Twinkler and shine as bright as I possibly can." On that very night, Little Star quietly slipped away from the Cluster family when nobody was looking. Whoosh... She soared up and up - as fast as she could without knowing where she was heading.

At last, she found herself in a magical land higher than she could imagine. Beautiful white fluffy clouds were slowly drifting by. A mysterious voice was softly echoing... "Little Star – my name is Lucile. I am a Twinkler and would love to teach you all about twinkling! Would you like to join me tonight"? Well, of course, Little Star was overfilled with joy and excitement. "Oh yes – that sounds wonderful" Little Star and Lucile twinkled together throughout the night.

Lucile smiled at Little Star and said, "Little Star, you are a natural." It made her feel happy and good inside. Lucile was a great teacher. Every night Little Star would quietly slip away from the Cluster family to join her new friend Lucile, and as she traveled up higher and higher, she would sing;

Sing! (To the tune of 'London Bridge's falling') Shining bright, that's what I do, in the sky, way up high. Shining sunny, that's what I do, no matter what they say! One night everything changed. Not long after Lucile and Little Star started twinkling, Lucile looked at Little Star. She called out in a grumpy voice, "Little Star, you should go back to your Cluster Family. I am swamped and cannot teach you anymore".

Little Star felt confused and did not understand why Lucile was so unkind. Trying hard to hold back her tears, Little Star flew back to the Cluster Family. She smiled on the outside but inside, she was feeling despondent. All of a sudden, her light stopped shining... The other stars in the Cluster family did not notice because they were in the middle of huddling. After what seemed a long night of crowding, Little Star had a visitor.

It was no ordinary visitor! Angelique, Guardian of the Dream Clouds, appeared from behind a pink feathery cloud. Angelique spoke. "Little Star, I have an important message for you. I have been watching you shine as a Twinkler. You need to know that you are the brightest Twinkler in the sky, and this is where you now belong if you wish"! Little Star was very excited. Angelique went on to say, "Little Star – look, your light is getting brighter and brighter"! Small Star looked in amazement and then understood that her light was only strong enough to shine as long as she believed in herself.

That's why it stopped shining when she felt sad and not good enough. Little Star also realized that Lucile was unkind because it made her sad to see Little Star's light twinkling so bright.

Little Star thanked Angelique and decided to follow her dream to shine as bright as she possibly could no matter what! She flew back to the Twinklers, feeling very strong and excited. In a happy voice, she sang;

 Sing! (To the tune of 'London Bridge's falling') "Shining bright, that's what I do, in the sky, way up high. Shining bright, that's what I do, no matter what they say"!

From that day forwards, Little Star was known as Bright Star, and she was indeed the brightest star you could ever imagine! Her job was to help others find their light and teach them how to be their most brilliant cheerful!

Nell Goes Shopping

Nell and her mom love to go shopping at the mall. Her mom always lets her decide what store that they visit and shop in. In case you didn't know, Nell is six years old. Her birthday is in June, and she will be seven then. Today Nell thought it would be a good day to go to O' Brian's Shoe Store because it is close to the ice cream store, and just maybe mom will buy her a cone of her favorite, peach and nuts. As mom and Nell pull into the parking lot, mom says to Nell, "Now Nell, remember where we park. You know that I forget sometimes." Mom only pretends to forget so that Nell will get used to remember things like that.

Once mom parks the car and Nell and her go into the mall, Nell starts looking into all the windows. Every store has something new and exciting to look at. One has clothes on dummies that look board and funny looking, while others have kitchen tools all shiny and bright.

Nell is having a great time. Mom and Nell go into O' Brian's Shoe Store, and Nell starts looking at all the dress shoes. "Mom!" she says. "Look at the pretty dress shoes." Mom smiles and tells her today they are looking for gym shoes for school gym class. "Oh, Mom." Says Nell. A young girl comes over and asks if she can help them, and mom says, "Yes, we would like a pair of gym shoes for Nell." "OK.," the girl says.

When the girl brings Nell her shoes, Nell tries them on, and they fit just right. Mom gets up and walks over to the line to pay for them. The bar is very long, and Nell starts to get bored. She wanders to the front door and looks out. Across the way, she sees a bookstore. Nell always likes to read books ever since she learned how. Nell runs across to the bookstore and looks in the window.

Then as Nell walks to the end of the window, she comes to the entrance. She looks back into the shoe store and sees that the line to pay is still very long; so, Nell decides to go into the bookstore and sees what's there. Nell starts to read a book that looks good, and the more she read, the more she wanted to read. Before she knew it, she had forgotten all about her mom.

Nell's mom paid for the shoes and took the bag from the girl behind the counter. She turned around and looked for Nell.

"Nell?" she called out, but there was so much commotion going on around her that she could not hear if Nell answered her call or not. Mom walked around the whole store but could not find Nell. She walked out into the hall and looked both ways—no Nell. Mom started to get worried and called out Nell's name again but still no answer.

Nell was still reading the book that she found and didn't hear her mother calling her name. Nell's mom saw a guard walking nearby and waved to him. "What's the matter, lady?" He asked. "I can't find my daughter Nell." The guard and mom walked back into the shoe store and looked all around, then back into the hall up and down a few stores on either side—no Nell. Nell got so sleepy reading that soon she was sitting on the floor and closed her eyes and fell fast asleep.

She was in a corner behind some shelves, and no one noticed her sitting there. Her mom and the guard went to the main office to report that Nell was missing and that all stores should be on the lookout for her. Nell's mom was anxious and described what Nell is wearing and her hair's size and color. Nell woke up and rubbed her eyes. "Oh my!" she said and jumped up. She ran out of the bookstore and into the shoe store and looked at the line of people paying for their shoes, but her mom was not there.

Nell started to be afraid and looked for someone to ask for help. She remembered her mother's warnings to not talk to strangers, but everyone in the store was a stranger. What should she do?

Nell saw the young girl that had waited on them, walked up to her, and said, "Did you see my mother leave?" The girl said that, yes, her mother had left quite a while ago. Nell told her that she thinks she lost her mom and that she needed help in finding her. The young girl took Nell to the front door.

There she looked left and right and asked Nell if she saw her mom. Nell looked and then said no to the girl. They walked back to the counter, and the young girl picked up the phone and called the guard post. The guard answered, and the girl told him about Nell. "Yes, we are looking for Nell, and her mom is here with me now. We will be right there." The young girl says to Nell, "Your mom will be here in just a moment."

Nell felt better when the girl said this. When Nell's mom returned to the store, she hugged Nell and then asked her where she had been. Nell told her about the bookstore and falling asleep. Nell's mom was glad to see her, but she said Nell should always stay close to her whenever they shop- ping just because of this. When they got to the parking lot, Nell said she was sorry and that it won't happen anymore. Then she pointed to their car, and mom and Nell walked over and got in and drove home.

Asad and the Colorful Butterflies

At the weekend, Asad went to visit his grandfather. The two days passed very quickly, and before Asad knew it, his father had arrived to take him home. Asad said goodbye to his grandfather and went to sit in the car. He was looking out of the window as he waited for his father to collect his things. A butterfly sitting on a flower a short distance away fluttered its wings and flew to the car window. "You're going home, aren't you, Asad?" asked the butterfly in a tiny voice.

Asad was astonished. "Do you know me?" he asked. "Of course, I do," smiled the butterfly. "I've heard your grand-father telling the neighbors about you." "Why didn't you come and talk to me before?" Asad inquired. "I couldn't because I was in a cocoon up a tree in the garden," explained the butterfly.

"A cocoon? What's that?" asked Asad, who was always a curious boy. "Let me explain from the beginning," said the butterfly as it took a deep breath. "We butterfly hatch out of the egg as tiny caterpillars. We feed ourselves by nibbling leaves. Later we use a liquid that comes out of our bodies like thread and wraps ourselves up in it. That little package we weave is called a cocoon.

We spend a while inside that package as we wait to grow. When we wake up and come out of the cocoon, we have brightly colored wings. We spend the rest of our lives flying and feeding ourselves from flowers." Asad nodded thoughtfully. "You mean all those colorful butterflies were once caterpillars before they grew wings?" "Can you see the green caterpillar on that branch?" asked the butterfly.

"Yes, I see it. It's nibbling away hungrily at a leaf." "That's my little brother," smiled the caterpillar. "In a while, he'll weave a cocoon too, and one day he'll be a butterfly-like me." Asad had lots of questions to ask his new friend. "How do you plan this change? I mean, when do you come out of the egg, how long do you stay as a caterpillar, and how do you make the thread to weave your cocoons?" "I don't plan any of it at all," explained the butterfly patiently. "God has taught us what we need to do and when we need to do it. We just act in the way our Lord wills."

Asad was impressed. "The patterns on your wings are wonderful. And all butterflies have different patterns, don't they? They are colorful and eye-catching!" "That's proof of God's incomparable artistry. He created us one by one in the most beautiful way possible," explained his friend.

Asad agreed enthusiastically: "It's impossible not to see the beautiful things God has created. There are hundreds of examples all around us!" The butterfly decided: "You're right, Asad. We need to give thanks to God for all these blessings." Asad looked over his shoulder: "My father's coming. It looks like we're about to set off. It was great to meet you. Can we talk again when I come next week?" "Of course," nodded the butterfly. "Have a safe journey home."

The Woodpecker and Henry

That Sunday, Henry went for a walk in the woods with his father. While he was walking, he was thinking about how beautiful the trees and all of nature were. His father then bumped into a friend, and as the two grown-ups were chatting, Henry heard a sound: Tap, tap, tap, tap, tap, tap... The sound was coming from a tree. Henry walked up to the bird that was making it and asked: "Why are you hitting the tree with your beak like that?" The bird stopped what it was doing and turned to look at Henry.

"I am a woodpecker, " it answered. "We make holes in trees and build our nests in them. Sometimes we store our food in these three holes. It is the first hole I've ever made. I will make hundreds more like it, though." Henry looked closer at the hole. "Fine, but how do you store food in such a small place?" he wondered. "Woodpeckers mostly eat acorns, and acorns are quite small," the woodpecker explained. "Inside each hole I make, I'll put one acorn. That way, I'll be able to store enough food for myself."

Henry was puzzled: "But instead of struggling with lots of small holes," he said, "you could make one big one and store all your food there." The woodpecker smiled: "If I did that, other birds would come and find my food store and steal my acorns. But the holes I make are of different sizes. When I put the acorns, I find them in the gaps, and I store them according to their size. The size of the acorn exactly matches the hole I put it into. That way, the acorn fits tightly into the hole.

Because God created my beak to take the acorns back out of the holes easily, I can take them from the trees without any problem. But other birds can't do that, so my food is safe. Of course, I don't have the brains to think all that out. I'm only a woodpecker. God makes me do these things. God taught me how to hide my food and Who created my beak in the right way for me to do it. It isn't just me—all living creatures can do the things they do because that is what God taught them."

Henry agreed: "You're right. Thank you for telling me all that... You reminded me of the great power of God." Henry said goodbye to his little friend and went back to his father. He was pleased because wherever he looked, he could see another of God's miracles.

Jacob's Big Surprise

On the first of June, it will be Jacob's sixth birthday. He is so excited because baseball has started, and he loves it so much he sleeps with the ball and glove his father gave him instead of the teddy bear his grandma gave him. The bear sits in the corner of his bedroom and gathers dust, but Jacob talks to it now and then, telling it that so and so hit a home run or about his little league game on Saturday.

He loves playing and watches it on TV whenever he can. His mother takes him to his games and watches from the stands. Jacob's friend is Charlie. He lives next door and is the same age as Jacob. Charlie also plays baseball with Jacob but is not as good. He likes to play hide and seek more than baseball and couldn't care less if he watches it on TV or not.

Charlie walked over to Jacob's house and knocked on the door. Jacob's mom opened the door and said, "Hi Charlie. What's cooking?" Charlie looked at Jacob's mom and shrugged his shoulders. "What does that mean?" he said. Jacob's mom laughed and said, "It means what is up." Charlie looked up and said, "The sky?" Jacob's mom laughed again and said, "Come on in. Jacob is in his room."

And Charlie walked over to Jacob's room and went in. "Your mom is sure funny." He said. "Why, what is so funny." Said

Jacob. "She asked me what was up, and the only thing I saw was the sky." Said Charlie.

"Let's go outside and throw this baseball around. It's too hot in here." Said Jacob. So, Jacob and Charlie went out the back door and into Jacobs's yard to play with the baseball. Jacob went to one side of the yard, and Charlie went off to the other. They threw the ball back and forth, all the while talking to each other.

"I have my birthday next week." Said Jacob. Charlie said, "I hope you invite me for some cake. Are you going to have some games?" he said as the ball went over his head, and he turned and ran it down. "I don't know. My mom takes care of that stuff. I hope my dad will be home from the Army soon.

Mommy said he might come home for Christmas. I miss him a lot." Said Jacob. Charlie's mom called to him for dinner, and so he left Jacob in the backyard with his baseball. Jacob watched Charlie go, then turned and tossed the ball in the air and caught it again. He did these five or six times, then threw it to the far end of the yard and ran after it. "It's no fun playing alone." He mumbled to his mom when he came in, and she asked why the sad face. "I can't play ball alone. Can you come out and play ball with me, mom?" he asked.

"Jacob, I have housework to do just now, but maybe after dinner, OK?" she said. When dinner was made and the dishes put away, Jacob, with his ball and glove in hand, stood by the sink until his mother was finished. "Now, mom?" he said as he looked up at his mother. "All right," she said, and with that, Jacob ran out the back door and down the stairs to the yard. "Yippy." He cried.

His mother came out carrying her husband's baseball glove and started to play catch with Jacob. Jacob was thrilled to have someone to play with, even if it is his mother. He would rather have his dad, but he knew that his father was thousands of miles away in the Army somewhere. The day came to an end, and Jacob got ready for bed. "Let's say our prayers, Jacob." Said his mom. Jacob knelt next to his bed and told his nightly prayers with the usual "And take care of daddy. Amen." In the end.

The next morning after breakfast was done, the doorbell rang. Jacob ran to the door, and upon opening it, he saw the postman. "Hi there, young fellow. I have a special delivery for someone named Jacob. That wouldn't be you now, would it?' he said. Jacob took the letter and said, "Thanks." And he closed the door. He ran to the kitchen and gave it to his mom. "It is a special delivery for you, Jacob. It's from daddy." She said.

"Can I open it, mom?" he said. Mom gave it to him, and Jacob opened it ever so carefully and looked inside. Out of the envelope came a letter and two tickets. Jacob's mom read the letter for Jacob. It said, "Happy birthday Jacob. Take these tickets for you and mommy and go to the ballpark to see a real game. Could you write to me and tell me all about it?

It when you get home again. Love Daddy." Jacob's mother had to turn around because of the tears coming in the wave as she read the letter. Jacob was so excited. He couldn't believe he was going to see a real game live for the first time. That night he said a special prayer for his dad. He couldn't fall asleep at first. The tickets were pinned to the corkboard next to his bed, and he looked at them until his eyes couldn't stay open anymore.

When the day came, Jacob and his mom drove to the ballpark. When she presented the tickets to the guard there, he looked at them and then said, "You have great seats. Right next to the dugout. Let me take you there." So, Jacob and his mom followed the guard and walked down to the seats next to the dugout. The game had not started yet, and the players were out in the field moving around here and there. Jacob was so excited.

He pointed to one player and then another all along, telling his mother who they were and where they played. He was excellent. As they sat there watching, someone came down their row and said, "Excuse me, I think that this is my seat." And he pointed to the seat next to Jacob. Jacob looked up, and there in front of him was his father. "Daddy!" he cried, and Jacobs's mother looked just as sur- prised. Jacob and his mother both stood up and hugged him.

Tears ran down everyone's faces, even those around them. When they looked out to the field, the players had gathered around in front of them and were clapping. "This is the best surprise birthday gift I ever will have." Said Jacob. His mother could only nod her head in agreement.

The Movie Star

One bright sunny day not long ago, a girl named Katrina came walking down the street in her town in the Midwest. Susan, a friend of Katrina, was walking the other way

when they met. "Hi Katrina," Susan said. "What's new?" asked Katrina. Susan was all excited. "Did you read in the papers that Jake Warner is coming to our town to make a movie?" Katrina said, "No, to our town?" "When? Where?" Susan said," He is coming tomorrow for try-outs." "I'm going to try out for a part in his movie." "Do you think I could come and try out too?" said Katrina. "Why sure, it should be a lot of fun even if we don't get to be in the movie." "Let's go to the mall to see if we can find some new clothes to wear to the try-out," said Susan.

"OK." Katrina said, "OK, let's go. So, Katrina and Susan went to the mall to see if they could find any new clothes. When they got to the mall, there were many of their friends there. The talk all afternoon was about the movie that was going to be made in their very own town. Katrina said to Susan, "Boy, there are so many kids that want to try out for this movie that I don't think that we have a chance." "I don't care, and I still want to try out." Said Susan.

The two girls went down the mall's fingers and stopped in almost every one of the fashion stores. They finely got tired and went home. Then they tried on all the clothes in their closets before deciding on what to wear. "I guess this will have to do."

Katrina said to herself because, by this time, Susan had gone home. The next day, Katrina got up and showered and dressed in the clothes she picked out the day before. "Well, I guess I'm ready." And out the door, she went. She walked down to Main Street, and when she came around the corner, she saw the line of kids waiting to go before the famous director. Katrina got closer and then saw Jake Warner.

He wasn't hard to make out with his wide brim hat and scarf around his neck. "Hey, over here," yelled Susan to Katrina.

Katrina saw her about halfway up the line. She got to her in a few steps and slid in front of her. A few girls gave them a dirty look, but Susan just stared at them, and they looked away. "How do I look?" asked Susan. "Just great," said Katrina. "I just know that you will get a part in this movie." The line moved slowly and time seemed to drag on until the girls were near the front.

A young man came to the front of the line and said. "Sorry folks, but it's late, and we have to break for today." There were moans and yelps from the people in line. But the young man wasn't finished. "So those who wish to try out tomorrow, I have some cards with numbers on them so that you can get back in the line at the place you left today. "and with that, I started walking down the line handing out cards.

Katrina took her card, and Susan and her left to go home, disappointed but hopeful. The next morning the two girls met again and had broken- fast at Susan's house. After breakfast, they took a walk to town and got in line using the cards they called the day before. "I hope that we don't have to wait too long only to be disappointed," said Susan. Katrina said, "Yah, that would be a bummer."

As the line got shorter, the girls moved to the front. When the young man finally came to them, he said, "Now don't try to do things on your own. Just listen to the director and follow his orders. OK?" The girls nodded and followed him into the old movie house. It was dark at first but soon, their eyes adjusted to the light, and they could see that many people were moving around.

"Come this way." said the young man. The girls entered the movie house, and inside, the lights were on, and some people were sitting in the middle rows about halfway back. "Alright, what's your name?" the director asked. Susan replied, "Susan." And then she was told to come up on stage. They told her to walk back and forth then asked her some questions.

Then that was that, and she was walking off the stage and out the door with the young man. "Next." Said the director. Katrina stepped up and walked up the steps to the stage. "What's your name?" the director said, and Katrina answered, "Katrina." They asked her some questions then they walk back and forth. The young man came over and started to walk Katrina off when the director called him over.

When he returned, he said to Katrina, "Can you come to the theater tomorrow at 1 PM sharp? Katrina said," Yes, I can." "Now, don't be late, we have a tight schedule, and we need to use our time wisely. If your late, you're out. OK?" Katrina nodded a yes and was shown out the door where Susan was waiting. "Well, what took so long?" said Susan. Katrina looked at her and almost screamed with joy, "I have to come back at 1 pm tomorrow. The two girls went home and told their parents all about it.

Katrina's mom was thrilled that her daughter would have a chance to be in a movie and not go to Hollywood. Dad was not as happy. He didn't trust the movie people. The next day, Katrina had to go to church because it was Sunday. After the service, the preacher came up to Katrina and said," Katrina, I need you to bring this basket to Mrs. Olson on the other side of town." Katrina was just about to tell him of her meeting at 1 pm when he said thank you and turned away to talk to someone else.

 It was only 12, and she had a whole hour, so she set off to deliver the basket. After giving Mrs. Olson the basket, Mrs. Olson insisted on giving Katrina some of her homes- made cookies. Well, Katrina couldn't say no to the old lady and waited for the cookies. "Thank you." She said and started down the street before Mrs. Olson could answer her. About halfway home, she was crossing the road near the fountain in the middle of town.

There had been a leak in a rush for years, but no one ever took the time to fix it, so the water ran down the street and made dirty puddles of mud here and there. As Katrina jumped over one, she slipped and fell right in the middle of the pool. By the time she got out of it and stood up, her dress was covered with mud. Katrina didn't know what to do and started to cry.

When she arrived home and looked at her watch, it was five to one, and her clothes were ruined. There just was no way she could change and still make it to the audition at the movie house on time. She laid on her bed and began to cry. Her mother came in to see what was wrong. "What's the matter, dear?" asked her mother.

Katrina only shook her head and cried louder. "I'll never get another chance in my life like this." she thought. About that time, Susan knocked on the front door to Katrina's house. "Is anyone home?" she said.

Director. Katrina stepped up and walked up the steps to the stage. What's your name? the director said, and Katrina answered, Katrina.

They asked her some questions then they walk back and forth. The young man came over and started to walk Katrina off when the director called him over. When he returned, he said to Katrina, can you come to the theater tomorrow at 1 PM sharp? Katrina said, Yes, I can."

Now don't be late, we have a tight schedule, and we need to use our time wisely. If your late, you're out. OK?

Katrina nodded a yes and was shown out the door where Susan was waiting.

Well, what took so long? said Susan. Katrina looked at her and almost screamed with joy, "I have to come back at 1 pm tomorrow.

The two girls went home and told their parents all about it. Katrina's mom was thrilled that her daughter would have a chance to be in a movie and not go to Hollywood. Dad was not as happy. He didn't trust the movie people.

The next day, Katrina had to go to church because it was Sunday. After the service, the preacher came up to Katrina and said, Katrina, I need you to bring this basket to Mrs. Olson on the other side of town. Katrina was just about to tell him of her meeting at 1 pm when he said thank you and turned away to talk to someone else.

It was only 12, and she had a whole hour, so she set off to deliver the basket. After giving Mrs. Olson the basket, Mrs. Olson insisted on giving Katrina some of her homemade cookies. Well, Katrina couldn't say no to the old lady and waited for the cookies. Thank you. She said and started down the street before Mrs. Olson could answer her.

About halfway home, she was crossing the street near the fountain in the middle of town. There had been a leak in a rush for years, but no one ever took the time to fix it, so the water ran down the street and made dirty puddles of mud here and there. As Katrina jumped over one, she slipped and fell right in the middle of the pool. By the time she got out of it and stood up, her dress was covered with mud. Katrina didn't know what to do and started to cry.

When she arrived home and looked at her watch, it was five to one, and her clothes were ruined. There just was no way she could change and still make it to the audition at the movie house on time. She laid on her bed and began to cry.

Her mother came in to see what was wrong. What's the matter, dear? Asked her mother. Katrina only shook her head and cried louder. I'll never get another chance in my life like this. she thought. About that time, Susan knocked on the front door to Katrina's house. Is anyone home? she said.

"Were upstairs, Susan," said Katrina's mom. Susan ran up the stairs and into Katrina's room. Katrina's mom was sitting on the bed next to her to find out why she is crying. "How come you not dressed yet?" Susan said. Katrina raised her head and said, "It's too late, it's after one, and they said I have to be there on time or I'm out."

Susan looked at Katrina and said, "Dah, it's only twelve-fifteen. Yesterday was the day to change the clocks." She laughed and poked Katrina. "Get up and change, or you will be late. Katrina moved as fast as she could and arrived at the movie house on time. "Thanks, Susan, she said and went inside. Susan waited and waited for the longest time when Katrina walked out with a sad face thirty minutes later.

Susan being the good friend that she was, said, "Don't think anything about this small-time stuff Katrina, you will be a star someday, I'm sure." Katrina couldn't hold it in anymore. "I was asked to be in this movie," she yelled. "I'm going to be a movie star." As Susan and Katrina ran all the way home to tell Katrina's mom and dad, they were yelling and hugging each other. Things will be changing for Katrina now. How much will only time tell?

The Scary Giant

Were upstairs, Susan said Katrina's mom. Susan ran up the stairs and into Katrina's room. Katrina's mom was sitting on the bed next to her to find out why she is crying. How come you're not dressed yet? Susan said.

Katrina raised her head and said, it's too late, it's after one, and they said I have to be there on time or I'm out.

Susan looked at Katrina and said, Dah, it's only twelve-fifteen. Yesterday was the day to change the clocks. She laughed and poked Katrina. "Get up and change, or you will be late.

Katrina moved as fast as she could and arrived at the movie house on time. "Thanks, Susan, she said and went inside. Susan waited and waited for the longest time when Katrina walked out with a sad face thirty minutes later.

Susan being the good friend she was, said, don't think anything about this small-time stuff Katrina, you will be a star someday, I'm sure.

Katrina couldn't hold it in anymore. I was asked to be in this movie. she yelled. I'm going to be a movie star. As Susan and Katrina ran all the way home to tell Katrina's mom and dad, they were yelling and hugging each other. Things will be changing for Katrina now. How much will only time tell?

Going on a picnic

Ronald is a six-year-old boy who likes to play with his friends from school. His best friend is Billy. Ronald's mom has just read a letter from the school asking for permission to go on a picnic the next day. Ronald says, "Mom, can I go please?" and mom says, "I have to ask your father first. So, mom goes to the garage and asks dad. "What do you think? Should we let Ronald go on the picnic with the rest of his class?" Dad looks at the paper and then at Ronald behind his mom.

"I suppose that it will be all right," he says. "Whoopee!" Ronald shouts. Then he runs back to his room. Mom shrugs and smiles at dad, then turn to walk back to the kitchen. Dad gets back to washing the car. Mom signs the form and puts it on the counter so that Ronald can take it in the morning.

The rest of the day, Ronald can only think of the field trip to go on a picnic the next day. He looks for his boots that he wants to wear. They are brown and have laces, which he still can't tie as yet, but he keeps trying. He finds a flashlight and puts it on the floor next to the boots. Then he pulls out his backpack and dumps out the stuff that is crammed in there.

Outfalls some stuffed toys he put in when he played big game hunter and a few plastic soldiers and a dinosaur. "There it is," said Ronald, and he picks up the dinosaur and throws it at a toy box, but it falls short and lands on the floor in front of the open lid. Ronald picks up the flashlight and puts it in the backpack.

He takes the toy soldiers and puts them in as well. When night time came, his mother walked into the bedroom and said to Ronald, "Ronald, put those toys away and get ready for bed. You have a big day tomorrow." Ronald moaned but picked up the stuffed animals and throws them into the toy- box. " I can't sleep. I have to get ready for the picnic." he said. 'Alright, settle down now and get your PJ's on." so Ronald got into his PJ's and came and said good night to his mom and dad.

As he lay there in bed before he fell asleep, his mom came in and tucked him in. "Good night, little man," she said and turned the light off and closed the door till it almost was all the way. There was a little light showing through.

Ronald was still afraid of the dark, so mom knew that the door should stay open just a little. Ronald tossed and turned a few times but soon, he was asleep and dreaming of his big day in the morning. Ronald is up early as usual, and his mom comes and helps him get dressed for the picnic.

She ties his big brown boots for him and takes his backpack out into the kitchen. There she makes him a sandwich and puts it into the pack along with some other snacks. She also puts two orange drinks in for him. Ronald puts the bag on and walks out to the front yard. There at the curb is Billy, his best Ronald is a six-year-old boy who likes to play with his friends from school. His best friend is Billy.

Ronald's mom has just read a letter from the school asking for permission to go on a picnic the next day. Ronald says, Mom, can I go please? and mom says I have to ask your father first. So, mom goes to the garage and asks dad. What do you think? Should we let Ronald go on the picnic with the rest of his class? Dad looks at the paper and then at Ronald behind his mom. I suppose that it will be all right. he says. Whoopee!" Ronald shouts. Then he runs back to his room.

Mom shrugs and smiles at dad, then turn to walk back to the kitchen. Dad gets back to washing the car. Mom signs the form and puts it on the counter so that Ronald can take it in the morning. The rest of the day, Ronald can only think of the field trip to go on a picnic the next day. He looks for his boots that he wants to wear. They are brown and have laces, which he still can't tie as yet, but he keeps trying.

He finds a flashlight and puts it on the floor next to the boots. Then he pulls out his backpack and dumps out the stuff that is crammed in there. Outfalls some stuffed toys he put in when he played big game hunter and a few plastic soldiers and a dinosaur. There it is, said Ronald, and he picks up the relic and throws it at a toy box, but it falls short and lands on the floor in front of the open lid. Ronald picks up the flashlight and puts it in the backpack.

He takes the toy soldiers and puts them in as well. When night came, his mother walked into the bedroom and said to Ronald, Ronald, put those toys away and get ready for bed. You have a big day tomorrow. Ronald moaned but picked up the stuffed animals and throws them into the toy-box.

I can't sleep. I have to get ready for the picnic. he said. 'Alright, settle down now and get your PJ's on. So, Ronald got into his PJ's and came and said good night to his mom and dad. As he lay there in bed before he fell asleep, his mom came in and tucked him in.

Good night little man." she said and turned the light off and closed the door till it almost was all the way. There was a little light showing through. Ronald was still afraid of the dark, so mom knew that the door should stay open just a little. Ronald tossed and turned a few times, but soon, he was asleep and dreaming of his big day in the morning.

Ronald is up early as usual, and his mom comes and helps him get dressed for the picnic. She ties his big brown boots for him and takes his backpack out into the kitchen. There she makes him a sandwich and puts it into the bag along with some other snacks. She also puts two orange drinks in for him.

Ronald puts the load on and walks out to the front yard. There at the curb is Billy, his best friend, with a pack of his own on his back. "Hi," says Billy to Ronald. Ronald gives Billy a wave and stands next to him at the curb. "My mom gave me a sandwich to take along," says Ronald to Billy. "Mine too," says Billy.

Before they can say anything else, the school bus comes around the corner and stops. The bus driver opens the door, and Billy gets on first. Ronald turns and waves to his mom, who is standing in the doorway waving back. Ronald climbs onto the steps and gets on the bus. He moves to the back and sits next to Billy, who is waving out of the window at his mom.

"This is going to be fun," says Ronald to Billy. "Yeah, I hope we see some wild animals," says Billy. Ronald looks at Billy and says, "Maybe a bear or tiger." "Are there tigers around here?" asks Billy. "I don't know, but I bet there are," says Ronald. "If I see one, I'll throw some rocks at it, and it will go away," he says.

The bus pulls away from the houses and moves on to another street to pick up some more kids. After a while, it goes to the school and comes to a stop at the front door. Ronald and Billy get off and go to their classroom and sit in their chairs. There is a lot of noise as the whole class is talking at once about the picnic. "OK, class, quiet down." The teacher shouts to them. Ronald turns to face the teacher. "I need those forms we sent home with you. "She says, and the class brings the forms up and gives them to her. "That's great. It looks like everyone is going on the picnic today."

The class starts to get loud again, and the teacher says, "OK, let's get in line so we can go out to the bus for our trip." Ronald and Billy get up first and are in front of the line when the teacher marches them out to the bus. They all get on with Ronald and Billy in the front seat. The bus pulls away from the school and starts down the road to the forest area where the picnic will be held. As the bus parks at the picnic area, Ronald and Billy are the first out and run to the tables set up for their picnic.

The teacher follows, and the rest of the children come with her. "All right, children, let's stay together now." The children's yells rise and fall as they run around playing tag and just having fun.

Ronald hides from Billy and then jumps out from behind a tree and scares him. "OK. Now it's your turn," says Ronald. Billy runs and hides behind a building not far away from the tables.

Ronald counts to ten, then turns and looks for his friend. The playing goes on for another hour. "I'm getting tired," says Billy as he walks back to the tables. Ronald watches Billy go to the table, where he takes his backpack off and sits down. Ronald shakes his head. "I'm not tired. I guess I will go and look for some wild animals in the forest." and so Ronald walks off to the trees, the friend with a backpack of his own on his back. Hi. says Billy to Ronald. Ronald gives Billy a wave and stands next to him at the curb. My mom gave me a sandwich to take along. says Ronald to Billy. Mine too. Tells Billy. Before they can say anything else, the school bus comes around the corner and stops.

The bus driver opens the door, and Billy gets on first. Ronald turns and waves to his mom, who is standing in the doorway waving back. Ronald climbs onto the steps and gets on the bus. He moves to the back and sits next to Billy, who is waving out of the window at his mom. It is going to be fun. says Ronald to Billy. Yeah, I hope we see some wild animals, says Billy. Ronald looks at Billy and says Maybe a bear or tiger.

Are there tigers around here? asks Billy. I don't know, but I bet there are, says Ronald. If I see one, I'll throw some rocks at it, and it will go away. He says. The bus pulls away from the houses and moves on to another street to pick up some more kids. After a while, it goes to the school and comes to a stop at the front door.

Ronald and Billy get off and go to their classroom and sit in their chairs. There is a lot of noise as the whole class is talking at once about the picnic. OK, class, quiet down. The teacher shouts to them. Ronald turns to face the teacher. "I need those forms we sent home with you. She says, and the class brings the forms up and gives them to her. That's great. It looks like everyone is going on the picnic today. The class starts to get loud again, and the teacher says OK, let's get in line so we can go out to the bus for our trip."

Ronald and Billy get up first and are in front of the line when the teacher marches them out to the bus. They all get on with Ronald and Billy in the front seat. The bus pulls away from the school and starts down the road to the forest area where the picnic will be held.

As the bus parks at the picnic area, Ronald and Billy are the first out and run to the tables set up for their picnic. The teacher follows, and the rest of the children come with her. All right, children, let's stay together now. The yells from the children rise and fall as they run around playing tag and just having fun. Ronald hides from Billy and then jumps out from behind a tree and scares him. OK.

Now it's your turn, says Ronald. Billy runs and hides behind a building not far away from the tables. Ronald counts to ten, then turns and looks for his friend. The playing goes on for another hour. I'm getting tired. says Billy as he walks back to the tables. Ronald watches Billy go to the table, where he takes his backpack off and sits down. Ronald shakes his head. I'm not tired.

I guess I will go and look for some wild animals in the forest. Ando, Ronald walks off to the trees a little way from the rest of the children. Ronald moves into the woods and pretends that he is in Africa like the books his mom reads to him. He wanders off and climbs onto a bolder, then up onto a small hill to see what he can see from there.

It takes some time, but he makes it to the top, and then, looking around, he sits down to rest. After a while, he gets up to go back, and as he moves his feet, his shoelace has come undone. Ronald tries to tie them, but he can't. He steps off to go back and trips over the laces rolls down the hill on the opposite side.

When he comes to the bottom, he tries to get up, but he has sprained an ankle and cannot stand. "Help!" he cries, but his voice doesn't carry over the hill to the teacher and the other children. He tries again and again, but it hurts too much. He starts to cry. Soon he is so tired that he falls asleep. The teacher calls the children together after they eat to go back to school on the bus.

When the bus comes, the children get on. Billy looks all around, but he can't find Ronald. "Teacher.." Billy says. "Ronald is not here." The teacher looks at all the children but sees that Ronald is nowhere to be found. "I will look for him," she says and leaves the children with the bus driver. She goes back to the tables and starts to call Ronald's name. "Ronald!" but there is no answer.

Meanwhile, Ronald wakes up, and now it is a little darker here in the forest. He moans because his ankle is sore and hurts when he tries to get up. As he sits back down, there is a noise from the bushes just in front of him. Ronald thinks about the wild animals he wanted to see. He pulls the flashlight from his backpack. "Will it be a tiger or bear." he thinks out loud. In front of him, the bushes part is a man dressed in green clothes and hiking boots.

"What have we here?" the man says to Ronald. Ronald looks at the man and then starts to cry. "Don't be afraid." the man says. "Are you hurt?" and Ronald shakes his head yes. "My ankle hurts," he says. The man comes over to Ronald and looks at his foot. "Oww," says Ronald and jumps a little. The man says, "You need to see a doctor. How did you get here?" he asks.

"I fell off the hill. We are on a picnic and ..." Just then, the man hears a woman calling. "Ronald!" "Is that your name, Ronald?" he asks. "Yes." Says Ronald. The man picks Ronald up and climbs the little hill. At the top, he sees the teacher. "Over here," he calls. The teacher saw them, runs to the mountain, and asks Ronald, "Are you OK, Ronald?" "I hurt my ankle," says Ronald. I can carry him. Where shall I take him?" the man asks. "Over to the bus if you will." says the teacher.

The man carried Ronald to the bus and sat him in the front seat next to Billy.

"What happened to you?" asked Billy when the man got off the bus. "There were wild animals after me and my little way from the rest of the children. Ronald moves into the forest and pretends that he is in Africa like the books his mom reads to him. He wanders off and climbs onto a bolder, then up onto a small hill to see what he can see from there. It takes some time, but he makes it to the top, and then, looking around, he sits down to rest.

After a while, he gets up to go back, and as he moves his feet, his shoelace has come undone. Ronald tries to tie them, but he can't. He steps off to go back and trips over the laces, and rolls down the hill on the opposite side. When he comes to the bottom, he tries to get up, but he has sprained an ankle and cannot stand.

Help! he cries, but his voice doesn't carry over the hill to the teacher and the other children. He tries again and again, but it hurts too much. He starts to cry. Soon he is so tired that he falls asleep.

The teacher calls the children together after they eat to go back to school on the bus. When the bus comes, the children get on. Billy looks all around, but he can't find Ronald. Teacher. Billy says. Ronald is not here. The teacher looks at all the children but sees that Ronald is nowhere to be found. I will look for him. she says and leaves the children with the bus driver. She goes back to the tables and starts to call Ronald's name. Ronald! But there is no answer. Meanwhile, Ronald wakes up, and now it is a little

darker here in the forest. He moans because his ankle is sore and hurts when he tries to get up. As he sits back down, there is a noise from the bushes just in front of him. Ronald thinks about the wild animals he wanted to see. He pulls the flashlight from his backpack. Will it be a tiger or bear? He thinks out loud. In front of him, the bushes part is a man dressed in green clothes and hiking boots.

What have we here? The man says to Ronald. Ronald looks at the man and then starts to cry. Don't be afraid. The man says. Are you hurt? And Ronald shakes his head yes. My ankle hurts. He says. The man comes over to Ronald and looks at his foot. Oww. says Ronald and jumps a little. The man says You need to see a doctor. How did you get here? He asks. I fell off the hill. We are on a picnic and ... Just then the man hears a woman calling. Ronald! Is that your name, Ronald? he asks.

Yes. Says Ronald. The man picks Ronald up and climbs the little hill. At the top, he sees the teacher. Over here. He calls. The teacher saw them, runs to the mountain, and asks Ronald, Are you OK, Ronald? I hurt my ankle. Says Ronald. I can carry him. Where shall I take him? the man asks. Over to the bus if you will. Says the teacher. The man had Ronald to the bus and sat him in the front seat next to Billy.

What happened to you? Asked Billy when the man got off the bus. There were wild animals after me, and I ran and tripped and hurt my ankle." said Ronald. "Wow." was all Billy could say. The teacher thanked the man, and then the bus drove back to the school. The bus left the school, and the teacher stayed on with Ronald. "I hope you will be OK, Ronald." the teacher said. When the bus got to Ronald's house, the teacher carried Ronald off the bus. Ronald's mom called to her husband, and the two of them met the teacher at the front door. After ex- plaining what had happened, Ronald's father looked at him and said. "I hope you have learned a lesson, Ronald."

Billy followed the teacher to Ronald's door and said, "He almost got eaten by a bear." Ronald's mom looked at Billy and told "Sure, Billy." Ronald and the bear's story were spread around the school the next day, and Ronald became a celebrity. He never said there wasn't any bear, and everyone thought not to ask.

CPSIA information can be obtained
at www.ICGtesting.com
Printed in the USA
BVHW090026140521
607263BV00002B/74